25-

3·14·88   746.8

Lindsey Donor 1940
Memorial Fund

12·3·87

In Memoriam

Lindsey Memorial Fund

Canvas Embroidery

Canvas Embroidery

Diana Springall

B. T. Batsford Limited London
Charles T. Branford Company
Newton Centre Massachusetts

© Diana Springall 1969

First published 1969
Library of Congress Catalog Card Number 69–10881

Printed and bound in Denmark by
F. E. Bording Limited, Copenhagen
for the publishers
B. T. BATSFORD LIMITED
4 Fitzhardinge Street, London, W.1, and
CHARLES T. BRANFORD COMPANY
28 Union Street, Newton Centre
Massachusetts 02159, U.S.A.

7134 2602 0

Contents

Acknowledgment

I owe special thanks to John Hunnex for the many hours of work involved in the photography of the plates, for which, with only a handful of exceptions, he is responsible, and for his tolerance and good humour when work had to be completed at short notice.

To all those who have generously loaned me work I am most grateful, for the book could not have materialised without their co-operation. I thank the Maidstone Museum for their warm-hearted help, the Victoria and Albert Museum for allowing me to photograph in their collection, and the Kunstgewerbemuseum Zurich for making a photograph for me.

To members of my family I express sincere appreciation for the many hours they have given to helping me.

I am grateful too to Constance Howard for giving her valuable time to looking over the almost completed work and to Anne Butler for her help and encouragement at the outset.

I am most grateful to Thelma M. Nye of Batsfords for her quiet confidence in the project at times when I myself felt the least confident.

D. S. Wrotham, 1969

Foreword

There has been a tendency up to now to reserve canvas work for traditional kneelers. It is the aim of this book to discover what canvas work has to offer and to show some of the many possibilities inherent in the medium. It has for too long been neglected and it is hoped that this work will serve to offer ideas for its revival for much wider uses and approaches. There is a need to revitalise and invigorate it in such a way that the all too common tendency to be content with slavish repetition of what others have done, can be replaced by personal exploration and expression, however simple. The photographs are not intended necessarily to suggest a final statement, but it is hoped that the various ideas will stimulate the reader to experiment and thus discover further the joys of this very old technique. The book is so planned that it will serve as a working manual for students and teachers and yet still be well within the capabilities of the beginner.

Introduction

A great deal has been said superbly by Constance Howard in her book, *Inspiration for Embroidery*, on the subject of inspiration for ideas in general. It is therefore not my intention to cover 'where to look', and 'how to look', in the same way, for this would be pointless. The purpose is to emphasise and assist in aspects of 'what to do when one has looked', but with canvas embroidery in mind, for a design cannot succeed unless it is entirely suited to the medium into which it is to be translated. In other words, to satisfy the demands of this medium one must think in terms of designing in areas and not in lines. Almost any subject or object is suitable for pattern making and it is the aim here to show how a selection of ideas, or things seen, can be put over in such a way that they do not become linear. There are many possible ways of putting the ideas on paper, using a variety of media, such as printing and cut paper which will help to express them and often give unexpected effects. These methods used with care could produce results advantageous to canvas work. It is hoped that by showing these connections with other media of two-dimensional expression, in addition to the more normal media of painting and drawing, new possibilities of designing will be opened up which have not been hitherto in any way linked with canvas embroidery. The advantages of these will certainly alleviate the worry for beginners in designing, for they need not be faced with graph paper and pencil!

In the photographs of work included in this book, a great range of approaches to canvas embroidery can be found from utilitarian projects, such as kneelers, to the full free expression of the medium in large wall-hangings. Area has been treated in a variety of ways from representational to abstract and there are countless new uses for traditional stitches.

The main emphasis is, however, on the enormous value of original thought, however simple the initial ideas, and to stress and prove that originality can be achieved right from the beginning. It is hoped that the book will prove that there is limited pleasure in pure technique and that the real pleasure and satisfaction lie in an individual and unique conception and that this, also, has a great deal more to offer to those who look at it. Not only should the design be 'yours', but the stitches should be used in an individual way. It is not a question of whether all the stitches are known to the embroiderer that counts, but whether one or two can be satisfactorily selected to fulfil perfectly a specific purpose in the particular project being undertaken.

Part 1   Projects

Thoughts on how to select and arrange shapes

There are many recognised methods of design which are based on mathematical divisions of a given area that result in a series of shapes or subdivisions which from the outset are related to each other. Some of these are briefly outlined here because they form one of the valid ways of understanding an area of paper or cloth. This facilitates and encourages awareness, not only of the motif upon an area, but also of the total area to be considered for design. In other words, it enables one to consider far more than just the pattern which is merely part of the whole. The background is as much part of the whole as the original subject matter and must be considered, divided, and embellished along with any other part of the panel.

Panel rectangulation

It is obviously not a necessity to divide one's chosen or determined area by mathematical methods, but these can often act as a guide when free inspiration is not naturally suggested by the subject for embroidery. For further reading see bibliography.

1   A selection of known methods of construction: panel rectangulation

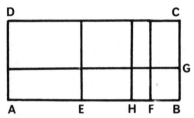

(a) Proportions and divisions are set up on all sides of the rectangle, all related to each other, and proper only to that rectangle. e.g.: DA is marked off on AB to give AE. AE = EF. FB is marked off on BC to give BG. EH = HB. Thus one can continue.

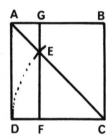

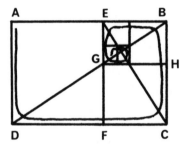

(b) Mark off CD on the diagonal of
            square CA. CD = CE.
      Therefore $\dfrac{CE}{DC} = \sqrt{2}$

(c) Taking any rectangle. From C extend a line to meet DB at 90° and extend to point E. Drop a perpendicular from point E to meet DC at F. The new rectangle, therefore, for consideration is the next rectangle EBCF. CE is the new diagonal and BG cuts this line at 90°. A perpendicular is dropped from G to point H and the new rectangle is EBHG and so on. Thus rectangles proportionate to each other and to the whole are created together with a spiral plan.

(d) Golden Mean Method. Given the rectangle ABCD. Mark the centre of DC say
at point E. Mark off CE on CB at point F.
Join FD. Mark off FC on FD, therefore
EC = CF = FH. Mark off DH on DC to
give point S. Erect a perpendicular from
point S to point G which is now the section.
Thus this can be applied to any of the
remaining three sides of any rectangle. It
could also be found by multiplying the
length of DC by ·618 and measuring from
point D along the base line.

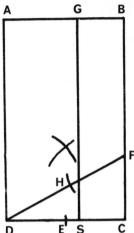

An area can be divided in a way that is as free as the mathematical
method is calculated. Two examples of completely free abstract
division are shown here to demonstrate the equally important concept
of controlled freedom; in these, no geometric calculations have been
used and yet the whole area in each case is satisfactorily divided. Both
have also been selected to illustrate the importance of pattern to
so-called background. It is in fact so important here and so far from
neglected, that it is not always easy to detect which are the applied
shapes and which is the initial area. Finally, the examples serve to
show the value of other media as inspiration for canvas embroidery.
The first is achieved by using cow gum to act as a 'resist' to the
printing ink or paint in one of many very simple methods of printing.
The second is the use of paper, cut or torn, to resist ink when using
either lino or silk screen methods of printing. Both form strong
patterns that use the whole area available and therefore could be
suitable, along with many others, for translation into canvas work
designs.

The many forms of printing offer countless suggestions for points
of departure. They so often contain a freedom and spontaneity that
allows a multitude of thoughts to flow beyond them into the realms
of canvas work.

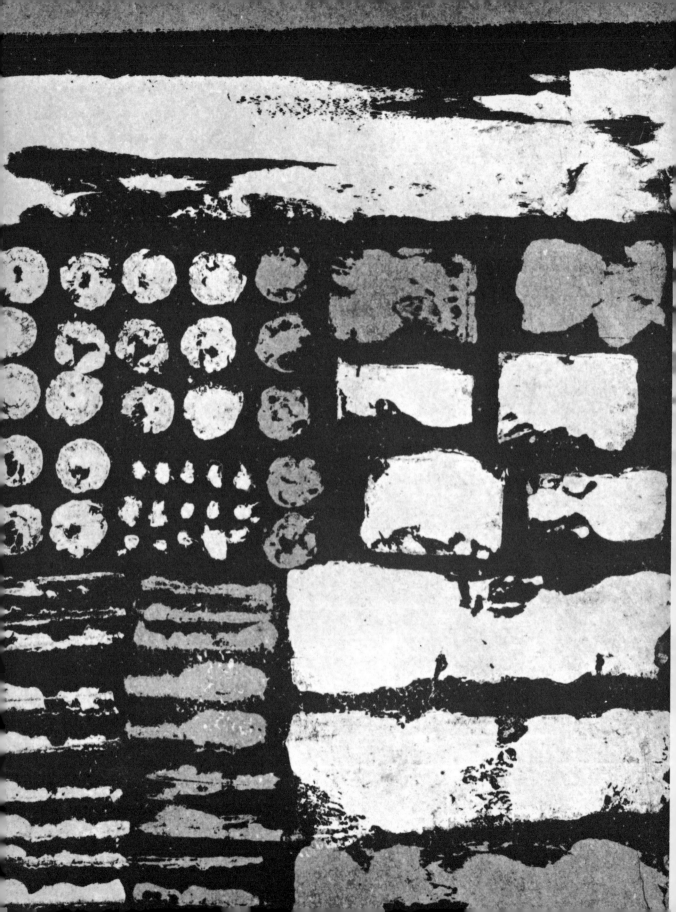

3   Print using paper as resist on silk screen   *Anne Parsons*

◄ 2   Print using Cow gum resist   *Roy Nott*

Another helpful way of breaking down what is seen around can be achieved through the medium of photography. Subjects suitable for canvas work are wide-ranging and unending. Much of nature is already a pattern for embroidery and the camera can very successfully capture and retain a collection of ideas that can be used in a countless variety of ways. The following photographs provide just a few examples of the variety of situations in which to search for attractive subject matter. They have all intentionally been given broad titles because each in turn offers scope for research into the many smaller aspects that go to make up these all-embracing collections of shape. The photographs, together with some line drawings, show how these can be taken further in terms of organisation for the purposes of this type of embroidery. Objects of this kind undoubtedly have great pattern value and these examples will, it is hoped, encourage the embroiderer to widen her searching grounds.

4   Sawn edges of logs ▶

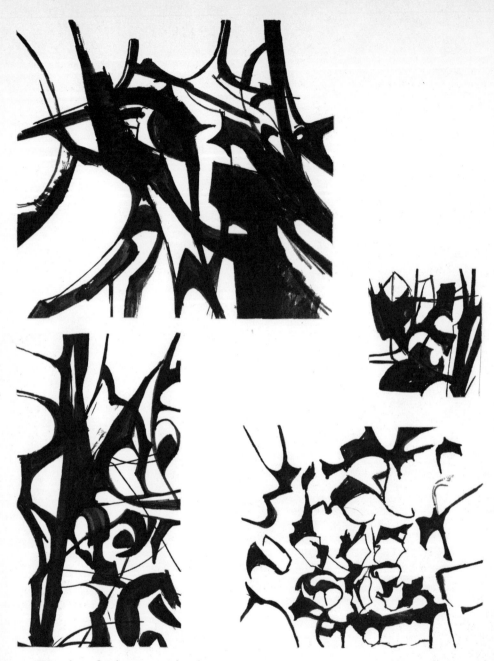

5   Drawings for interpretation into canvas work

6   View up into a tree ▶

Most subject matter offers many ideas when translated on to paper, but there are also ways of depicting things seen by using conventional tools in an unconventional way. A well-loaded brush of thick paint is more easily manipulated than pen and ink in depicting simple natural shapes and objects. With the same brush and different handling a slice of cucumber may appear as many things, each aspect sharing some of its qualities but each one, a variety of brush strokes giving a simple uncomplicated drawing. Almost anything could be approached or assessed in this way. A simple painted line is illustrated here and with it is shown a free unorthodox treatment of canvas work. Thick white rya rug wool has been combined with black perlé on a rug canvas ground from which some central shapes have then been removed to expose areas of black velvet inserted from the back.

9   Line with paint and brush   *Diana Springall*

◄ 7   Sawn branches
  8   Flint wall

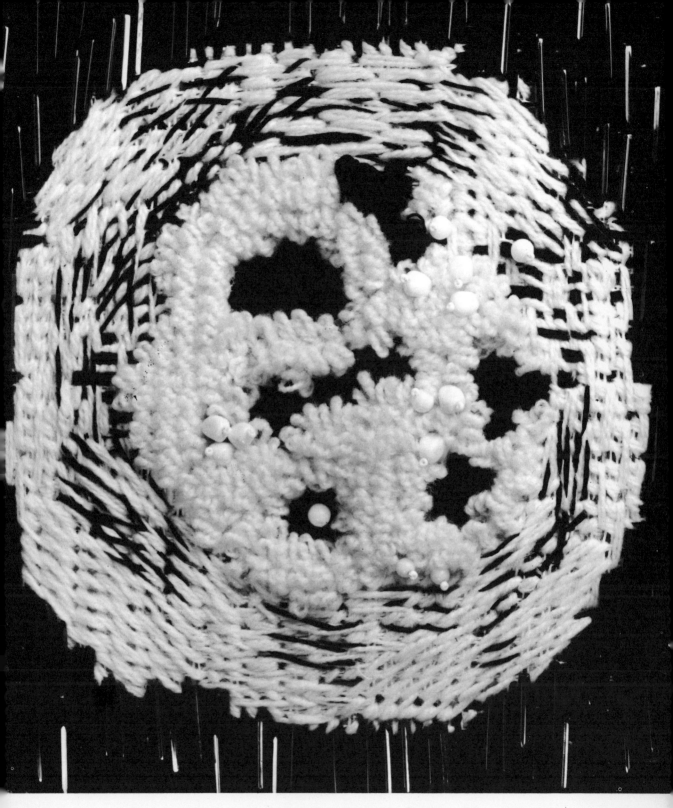

11 Cucumber in black and white   *Diana Springall*

◀ 10   Design of cucumber

23

Most traditional media can be rewarding. Charcoal is one that offers considerable freedom, for it must be used boldly. The accompanying sketch of a single flint serves to show how easily it may be adapted to suggest the broad areas of shape necessary for successful canvas embroidery. It also provides an example of how photographs such as those that appear earlier in the book could be further broken down and analysed.

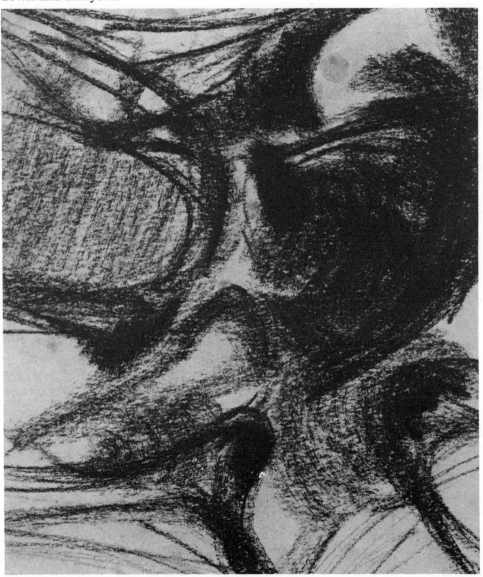

12 Charcoal drawing of a flint *Diana Springall*

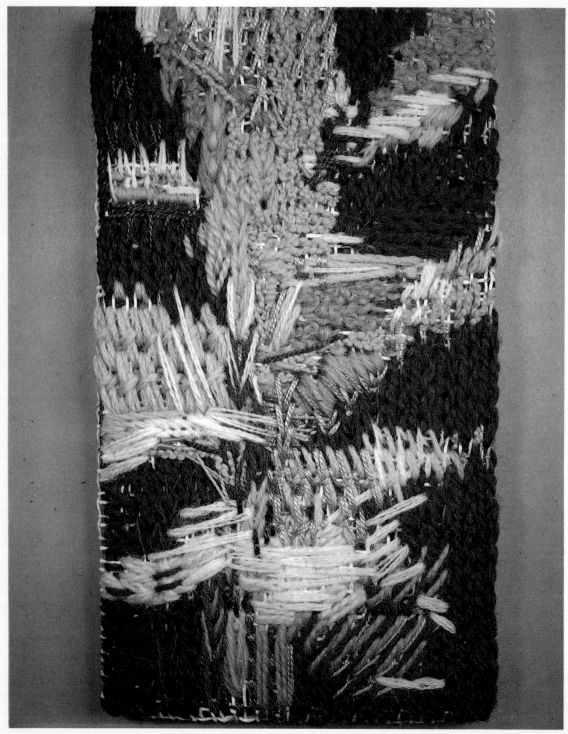

Weed Panel by Diana Springall

Another fascinating experiment, using conventional materials in a different way, was made with an enormous weed measuring over six feet high. The very large scale of the plant suggested oil paint on paper, so that the directional texture, clearly visible on the plant, could be retained in the design. The thickness of the paint also played a part in that it gave an impetus to the free treatment of the panel. The design was worked on a rug canvas in a variety of wools, from crewel to that used for ordinary knitting.

13   Weed in oil paint on paper   *Diana Springall*

Pencil and water-colour can be used in many ways but when used in an honest piece of research, such as the drawing opposite, its value is immense. From the drawing came the following simplified arrangement of the flowers for a design for the re-covering of a mid-Victorian chair (see pages 83–5).

14 Design for mid-Victorian chair *Annette Firth*

15 Drawing of convolvulus *Annette Firth*

Landscapes afford an unending source of pleasure and three simple initial studies are shown here, together with a piece of canvas embroidery which owes its beginning to many sketches such as these, and shows very simple distribution of shape. It is carried out on hessian and this ground fabric is allowed to play an important part, with a free use of traditional stitches, such as cross and double cross, in crewel and tapestry wools, together with beads.

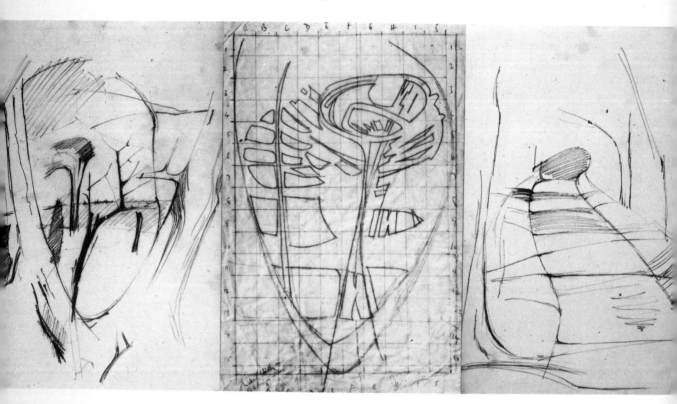

16   Three drawings of a simple shape in landscape   *Diana Springall*

17   *View Through a Divided Tree*   *Diana Springall* ▶

28

As with other forms of expression, cut paper offers great facility. To begin with, there are so many kinds of paper, from newsprint to brightly coloured tissues. The two ideas offered here as a basis for continued experiment and arrangement are in types of paper that are almost always readily available in every home. Newsprint alone has enormous possibilities. In the example shown here dark tones have been cut from part of an advertisement, and, while the movement of the three figures has been retained they have been so arranged as to give interesting shapes between each and also comfortably to divide and use the whole rectangle. The ways in which shapes may be acquired for inclusion in design are a thousandfold, and it is necessary to strive to achieve a collection of shapes that are pleasant to look at. This, however, is not enough; in nature, shapes miraculously go together in such a way as to form a harmonious relationship, and therefore, similarly, shapes may be related one to another in design.

18   Cut shapes from a newspaper advertisement

30

They need not, of course, look exactly alike but some slight characteristic common to each is a great help. These shapes cut from the advertisement each have something in common with the others. Similarly in the other example of lettering (this may be cut from any publication provided the letters are all selected from the same size and kind of type), certain common characteristics greatly ease the task of arrangement on another piece of paper. The ability to arrange shapes in a satisfying way comes with practise and is well worth the effort because it is the whole basis of the initial success of the project. With the first of the two newspaper designs, the dispersal and position of the three main tones has also been decided at the same time. No canvas embroidery is shown here as a direct result of these suggestions but the two seem without doubt to offer very many ideas for designing stall cushions, kneelers, etc. Both reiterate and stress the importance of the remaining area of space around the initial positive statement.

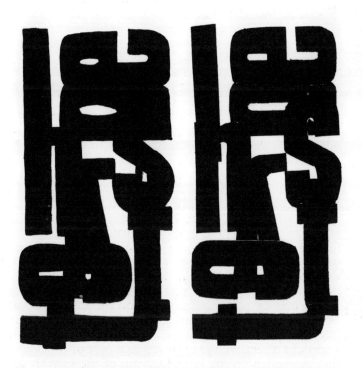

19   Lettering cut out and arranged to form a pattern

Thoughts on the selection of colour

Ideas on how to select shape and how to combine one with another to give a pleasing whole have been briefly outlined, for there are no hard and fast rules on how to achieve this. It is largely a question of looking and practising and discovering again and again. So, too, there are no rules on how to select good or pleasing colour. Once again there are plenty of scientifically calculated bases and approaches which can be studied in books in any library. The purpose here, however, is to show how the colour of something seen around may be incorporated with a design for canvas embroidery. Alternatively, one or two basic ways of thinking in terms of colour show how schemes can be invented if desired.

The natural or local colour of any of the subjects to be dealt with, provide a wealth of schemes that often need only selection or rejection. Those colours that are chosen as making a suitable combination have then to be apportioned and placed. Colour for the moment can once again be likened to the arrangement of simple pattern in that questions arise such as, should the darkest patches of colour be on the outside and what size should they be; should the most striking colour take a position somewhere near the centre or somewhere else? Nature can suggest colour combinations, but they must be worked on by arranging and re-arranging.

The variety of thickness and type of wools may be taken into consideration at the same time. Paint is one method of putting down on paper the combinations and quantities of colour the particular subject has to offer. However simply this is done does not matter, nor does it matter whether the paint is applied thickly or not. Posters, oils, acrylic and so on, all have their own characteristics. Posters are particularly easy as countless alterations may be made, often to advantage with the increased subtlety of one colour over another. Most paints can be used completely freely, piled up thickly or scratched or textured on the surface in numerous ways to achieve the quality and feeling of the work desired. It is essential to plan every aspect of designing for canvas embroidery to the last detail of colour, for most of the techniques are slow and too time-consuming to permit constant unpicking. The canvas work panel of *Three Flowers* was developed from colour that was initially suggested by the actual flowers themselves. Poster paint was freely moved about the paper to decide on final placing of colours and the amount of each colour to be used. Stitches were not suggested on the painting but were selected during work according to the directional growth of the plant, e.g. if a straight direction was required in a part of the flower, then a stitch that depended on the straight grain of the canvas, such as parisian, was selected. The colour of the flowers was of a considerable range and it was therefore decided that an entirely plain background would be required. To do a dull time-consuming quantity of this would be pointless so each motif was mounted separately on a dark brown hessian ground.

32

Morning Water   Hanging by Miriam Sacks
See page 43

20   Sketch for *Three Flowers* panel   *Diana Springall*

21 *Three Flowers* panel   *Diana Springall*

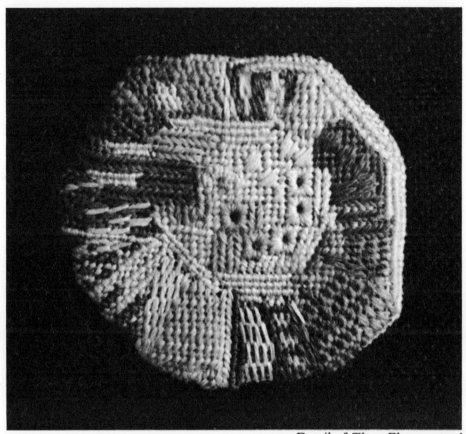

22   Detail of *Three Flowers* panel

The flower of an artichoke was another example where nature determined and suggested the first thoughts on colour, and in practice it will be seen that the local colours were merely brought up in key. Various drawings in pencil and colour led to this experiment in a variety of unusual wools. It is worked on a jute ground, where once again the background areas are left uncovered and wools have been selected that bear some considerable colour and textural relationship to the ground fabric. The stitches are traditional ones but used in an unconventional way, e.g. Bernat Klein wool used as tramming and then left without the next usual set of top stitches. Perlé and two-ply knitting wool have been used for such stitches as eastern.

23 Drawing of *Artichoke* panel *Diana Springall*

Artichoke Flower Panel by Diana Springall

24   Sketch for *Artichoke* panel   *Diana Springall*

Inspiration for designing with colour can come from mood. In other words, selection of colour can be something which has an association in the mind for a particular subject to be depicted. This is expressed in the detail of the panel of a *Stalactite Cave*, opposite, in which subtle changes of rich tones of purples and purple-browns are dramatically combined with brilliant yellow and white areas. A black and white photograph is also included to show how the entire area has been considered and divided into projections, cavernous depths and so on. Several stitches are used but padded straight gobelin and knotted predominate.

Page 39
25 *Stalactite Cave   Marjorie Cox, Maidstone College of Art*

Detail of *Stalactite Cave* Panel by Marjorie Cox

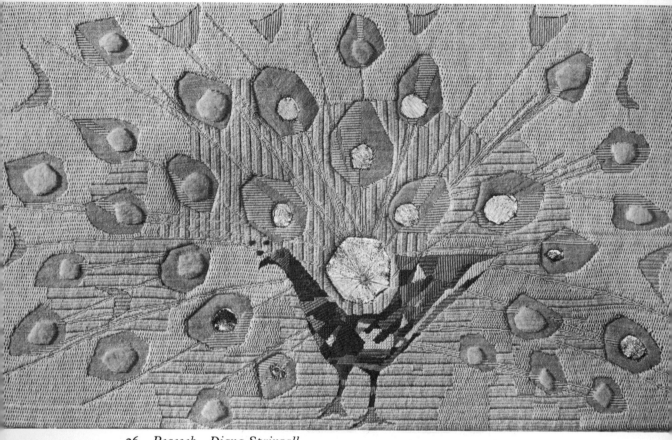

26 *Peacock   Diana Springall*

Colour can also be suggested and used in ways that have nothing in common with the local colour of the object and need have little connection with the mood created by the subject.

The panel of the peacock falls in this category for none of the colours necessarily suggest the real bird. This work was conceived mainly to stress the value and possibility of restricted colour in canvas work. It also serves to show that there are many openings for interest even if white only is used. In this case a low relief panel is achieved in the feathered tail simply by (i) altering the weight of the wool between rya rug wool and crewel, and (ii) by altering the stitch between gobelin and tent and in some cases velvet as well, but when only a small change of light was required, merely the direction of the tent stitch was altered. The tail areas with the higher relief, in other words those lying nearest to the bird itself, were achieved by working the shapes on a separate frame and letting them in from the back of

40

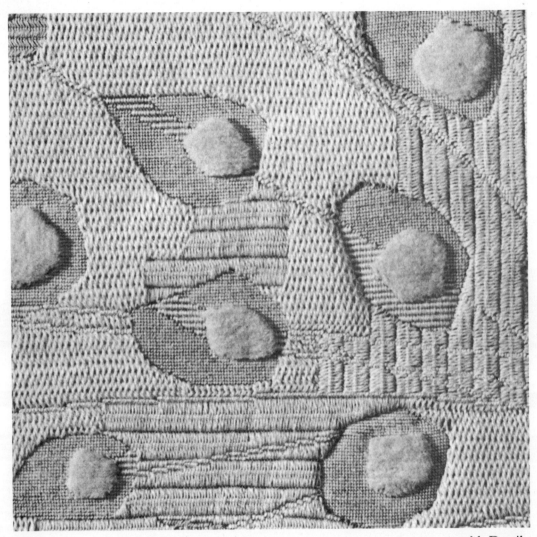

27   a and b Details

the main body of the panel. The outer tail feather shapes have a much lower relief, obtained by change of stitch and wool. Gold kid has also been inlet to carry the richness of the bird outwards. The veins of the feathers are worked in a pale pink again to carry something of the bird, in this case the hue, to the extremities of the rectangle. The work has, however, not entirely succeeded. The panel would be more successful if the range of pinks of the body of the bird had been kept to the pale pink of the veins of the feathers.

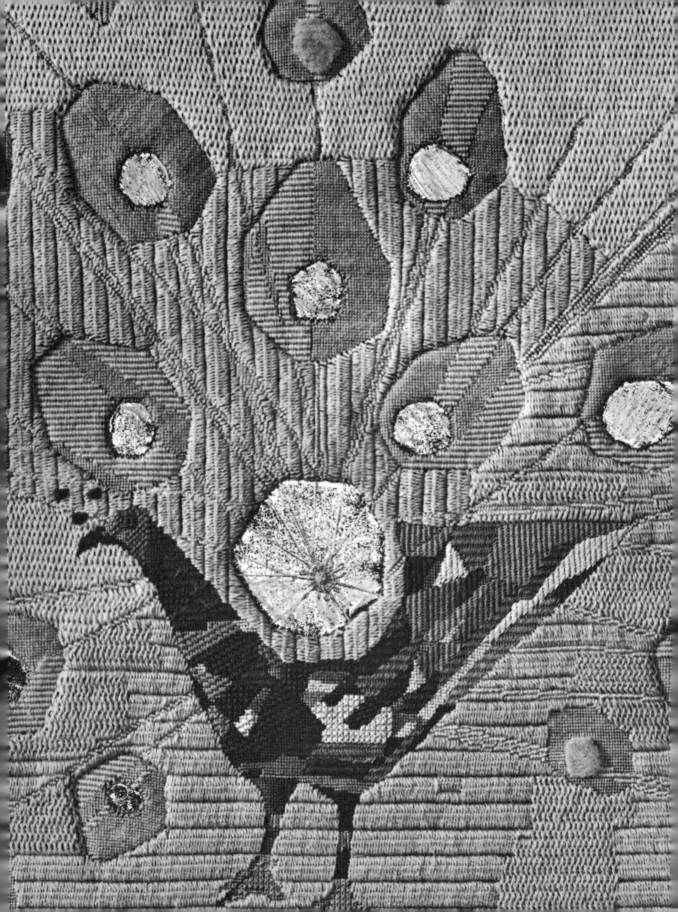

Summer Garden   Panel by Diana Springall

A country garden in summer suggested the colours and their quantities for the facing illustration. They are selected partly from memories and partly from an imagination of what the atmosphere of colour would be. Back stitch together with Bernat Klein and Fresca wools dominate the panel. The freedom and simplicity of the technique were sought to express the gaiety and joy of a simple scene.

An artist whose colour selection is entirely spontaneous and direct is Miriam Sacks, whose large hanging, *Morning Water*, is seen facing page 32. Without apparent scheme, the work progresses at great speed in a free, painterly manner.

The design from bark, facing page 44, was not related to the true colour of the subject, but was selected by placing together wools that were already in stock, and designing on paper with these and the initial studies in view. Quantities and positions of colour areas gradually found their place after arrangement and re-arrangement. The whole comprises a circle mounted on a dark hessian ground and was started with the aim of experimenting solely with florentine stitch which has been employed throughout except for occasional use of back stitch and satin stitch.

Stitches and how to select them

The selection of stitches, as in all the other parts of a project, depends a great deal on personal likes and dislikes and on taste in general, but an important function of stitchery lies in its ability to contribute to the work the particular effect desired and this can basically influence their choice. The accompanying photographs show how a range of approaches have been employed.

1 *Their most simple uses*
A great variety of stitches need not be included to produce an interesting or successful work. A limited selection can give great richness of movement, pattern and texture, even when only one colour is used.

The following seven photographs show this in practice. In five of the examples, only two stitches have been used and in some cases these have been carefully combined with beads of a shape that link with the character of the stitches. In each case they have been worked in one colour. Richness of texture and light and shade, and the varying heights of relief have been achieved by careful, simple and uncluttered selection.

28–34 Samplers worked by students at Maidstone College of Art

Tree Bark Panel by Diana Springall
See page 43

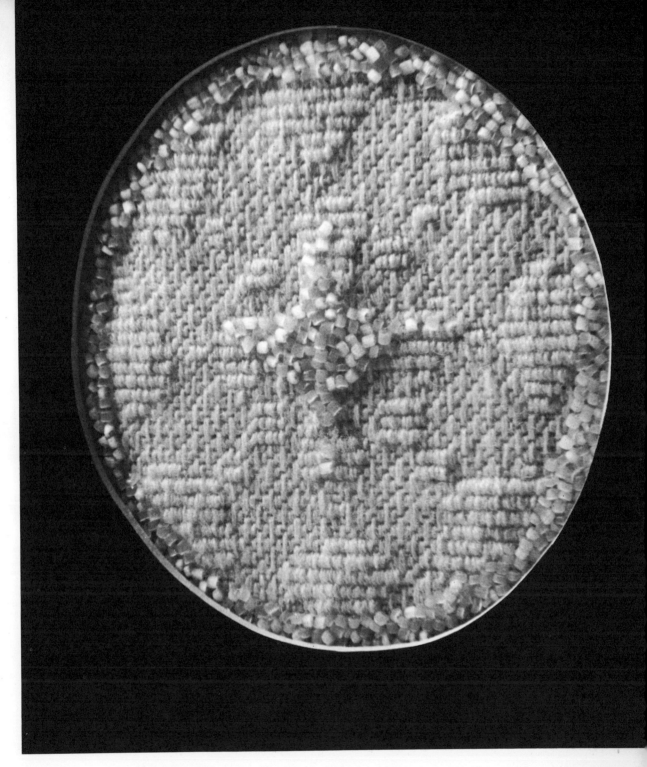

28 Renaissance with a variation of parisian stitch together with short
bugle beads

29　Velvet and tent stitches combined to show fairly high but simple relief

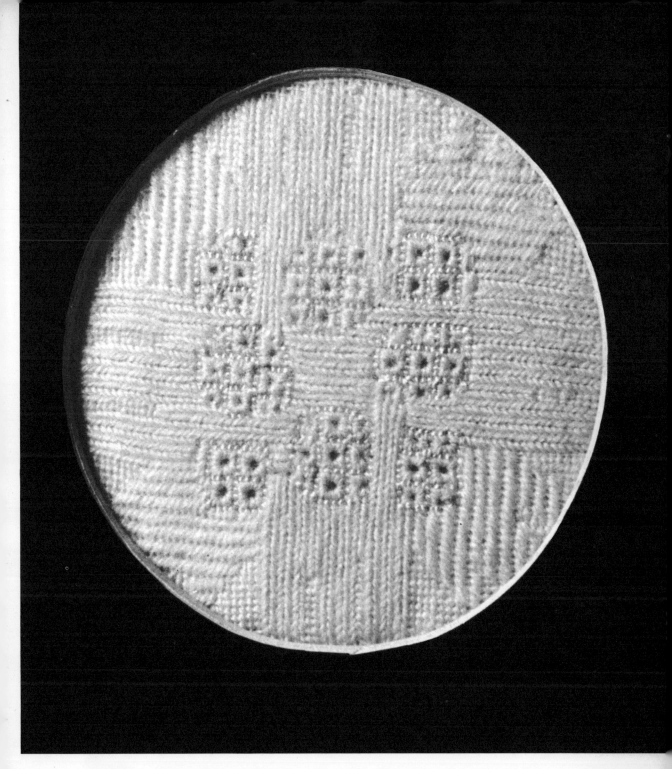

30 Wide gobelin, knitting, eyelets and a little tent stitch, show a low relief sample that contains, nevertheless, a variety of tone

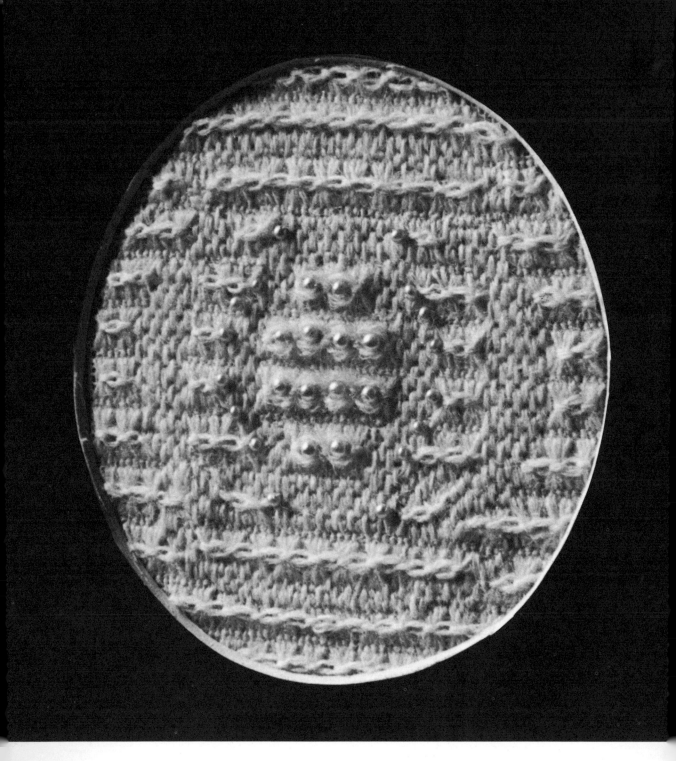

31 Here upright gobelin is used with shell stitch. In the central areas the
last stage of the shell stitch has been carried out rather more loosely
to allow a circular hole to be left where a pearl has been placed

48

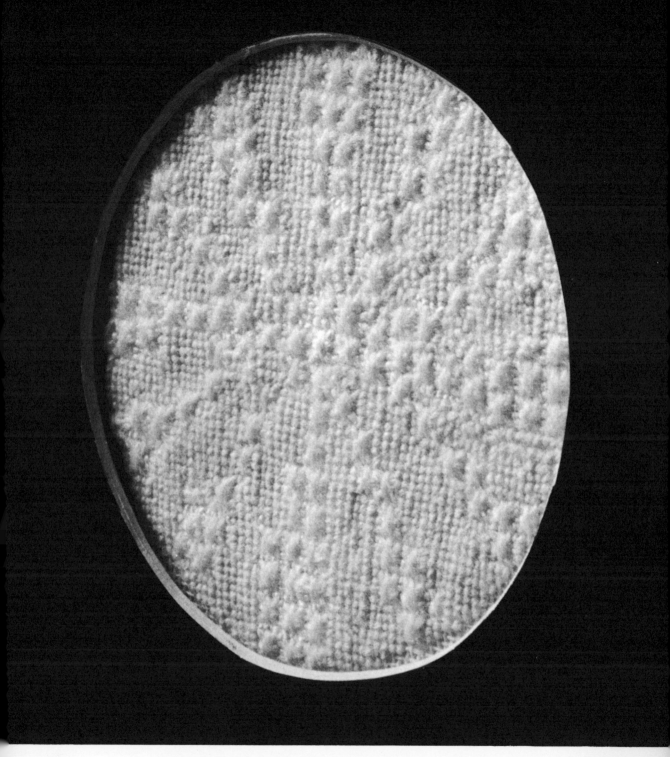

32 Cross stitch and double cross stitch have been combined to give a flat but interesting texture

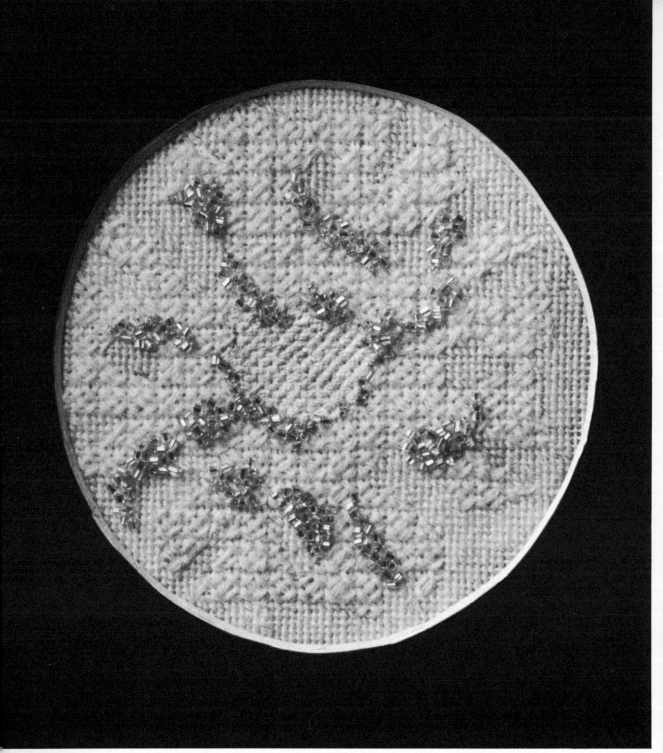

33　Rice, tent, and rococo stitches have been used in conjunction with small glass beads of a darker tone. The patches of beading reiterate the shapes already stated in the embroidery

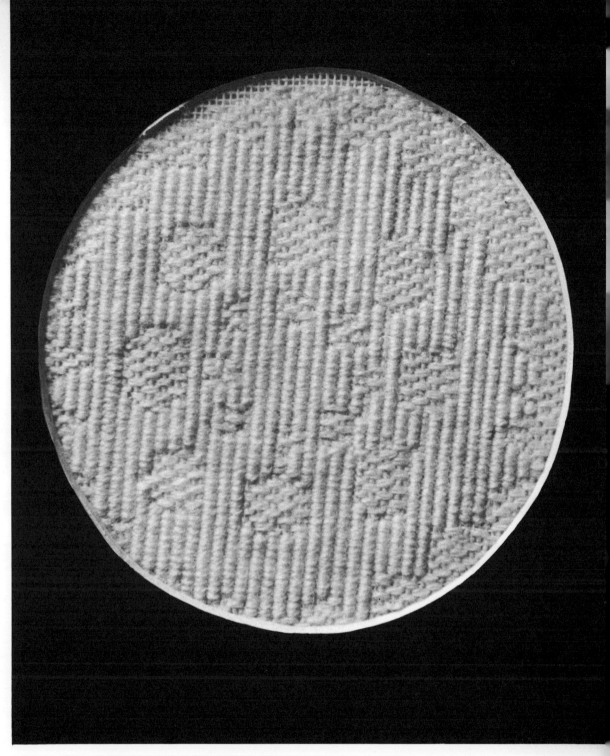

34 Straight gobelin, padded, together with parisian stitch provides ideas
for a rich but very simple surface

2 *Their uses when employed in greater number*

A greater range of stitches is often desirable and can be necessary as well as valuable in various projects. An example of this is provided by *Halved Pepper*, in which the use of different types of stitch helps to convey more adequately something of the variety of texture and pattern of the actual object. The stitches, and their positions and quantities, have been carefully selected according to the scale required to achieve certain effects; for instance, in the intricate central areas a small stitch is used in contrast to bold, larger scale stitches towards the outside. An increased sensation of texture and pattern is brought about also by the variety of threads used. Perlé, stranded cotton, rya rug wools and crewel wools have all been used to add to the richness. In order to prevent the whole from becoming over-complicated, the fabric on which the shape is mounted has been allowed to show through. The canvas has been cut and turned in, so giving plain areas on which the eye can rest.

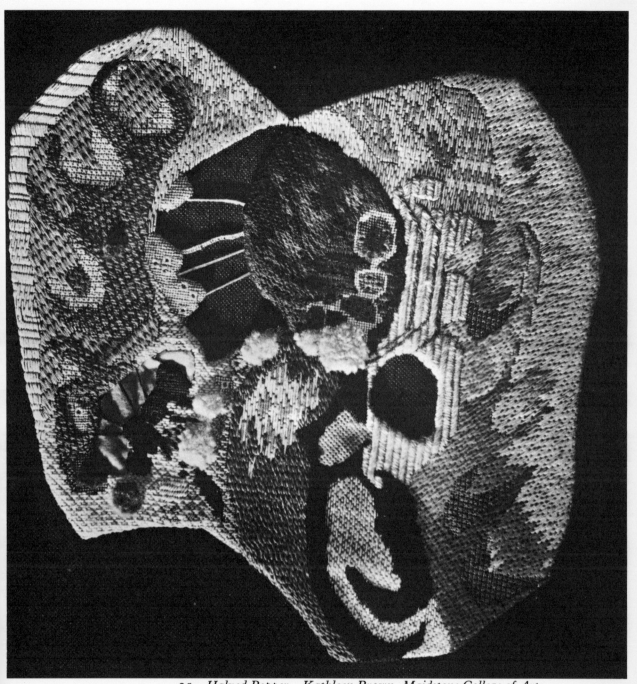

35   *Halved Pepper   Kathleen Brown, Maidstone College of Art*

36 *Brussel Sprout   Susan Legg, Maidstone College of Art*

Two other examples are given to show the value of using a range
of stitches. The first is a study of a *Brussel Sprout*, in which the texture
and direction of the stitches have been selected to correspond to some
of the movements and implied directions of the complex shapes of the
object itself. The surrounding area is treated in an original use of
couching on canvas, which, by its very character, continually leads
the eye back to the central motif.

38 *Flower   Brenda Gurton, Maidstone College of Art*

The second shows a rich combination of patterns where a variety of stitches was necessary to give movement to the shape. The motif is in brilliant colours and the variety of stitches, although of a non-dominant character, adds to the excitement and movement of the panel as a whole. The complete motif has been set into a tweed ground chosen for its textural woollen quality akin to the canvas work.

The use of greater numbers of stitches is possible when an isolated motif is used, but is also important for areas and spaces around and between motifs where they can be used to relate one part of the work to another. The panel of a simple *Flower* has a vertical emphasis in composition which has been assisted by the use of a knitting stitch, also vertical in character, in the surrounding areas. The flower and the total area in which it rests are, as a result, a complete unity. Colour has also prevented the two parts from becoming separated because the whole of the area relegated to knitting stitch has been broken up by varying amounts of similar colours of the main idea which was not conceived alone and unrelated to the space around it; the background was not produced mechanically as an afterthought, but worked alongside the motif at one and the same time. The stitches on the flower itself have been selected to show and suggest the intricacy of the central areas and the direction of growth of other parts.

◀ 37   *Flower   Betty Cowie, Maidstone College of Art*

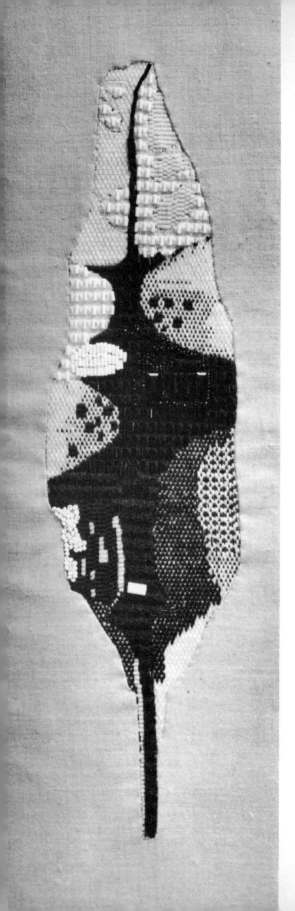

3 *Stitchery that can, with simple variation, change work tonally*

In the following example of *Grass in Space*, the space is as important as the grass itself. Parisian stitch proves to be most versatile. It is first used only in white in the top left of the work and is then translated into a combination of white plus black in varying proportions elsewhere, thereby creating completely different weights of tone. Shell and renaissance stitches have also been used in conjunction with black and white beads of a similar character to the stitching. A detailed photograph shows rectangular and bugle beads in conjunction with shell stitch. With this, as with other previous examples, a heavier stitched background would have been unnecessary and clumsy. The fine hair canvas into which it has been set, allows the complex collection of texture a chance to be read.

39 *Grass in Space   Diana Springall*
40 Detail of *Grass in Space* ▶

4 Stitches and their uses for pattern

Stitches can also be selected for their decorative contributions. The following three plates by pupils at Bromley Grammar School show this admirably. The surrounding areas have in each case been treated with as much love and thought as the subject matter itself, and take on a character and originality of equal importance. Two of the panels depict a living creature and the environment of each is as rich in pattern as the main motif and yet does not supersede or dominate it.

The detail of the panel depicting *Two Lizards* shows a lively sense of rhythm in the division of the area as a whole and some of the most dominant shapes of the main motif are emphasised again in the foliage and fauna behind. Each of many parts of the total picture, therefore, has its own pattern and individual richness but all are held together by shape. The lizards do not lose their identity amongst the variety of pattern because they have been worked in colours that have a greater light saturation than those of the background.

41   Detail of *Two Lizards*   *Sandra Town, aged 16/17, Bromley Grammar School*

42   *A Cat   Pupil aged 16/17, Bromley Grammar School*

Dominant background patterns are apparent in the picture of *A Cat*. The horizontal mass of the creature is challenged by the vigorous pattern of the vertically-placed trees, which have their obvious uses in contributing to holding the whole composition together, but do not deny the cat the position of greater importance.

62

43   *Fruit   Alison Blythe, aged 14, Bromley Grammar School*

Fruit has been included to show how dominant patches of pattern can be linked by means of simple bands of stitchery together with a little couching.

5 Stitchery combined with other forms of embroidery

Canvas work offers many possibilities of combination with other forms of embroidery. A beautiful example of this is shown below and in the detail opposite where rich shapes of padded velvet and hand-made cords are delicately linked by the intricacy of tent stitch. A pleasing awareness is displayed of the importance of a simple small-scale stitch that has been perfectly selected for the task it performs.

44   *Bark   Molly Arnold*

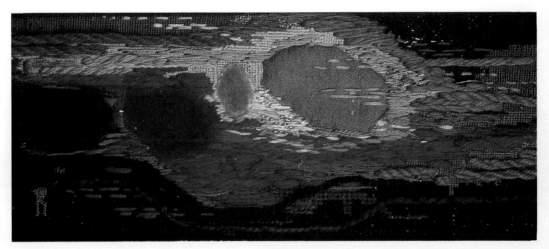

Detail of *Bark*   Panel by Molly Arnold

6 *Further uses of stitchery*

At this stage it can be seen that the possibilities and variations in the application of canvas embroidery stitches are infinite. One factor does, however, seem boldly to divide this whole field of experiment into two parts. All the work in this book is linked in some way, whether by a slender and tenuous connection or by a feature that is direct and obvious, with traditional canvas embroidery of the past. The main distinction, however, lies between the use of canvas work for practical and utilitarian purposes (e.g. in the making of three-dimensional objects such as bags, chair seats, etc.) and its use for purely decorative purposes with which can be combined endless ideas for interesting experiment.

Practical uses of stitchery

In this section originality of approach must be tempered by a certain degree of orthodoxy in so far as certain restrictions may be imposed by the purpose which the finished article is intended to serve, e.g. large long stitches or huge beads, being uncomfortable to sit or kneel on, would for obvious reasons be unsuitable for cushions or kneelers. The most hard-wearing stitches are those that have a complete integration with the background. In other words, are not surface decoration, and it is these that are the most suitable for articles subjected to continuous wear. However, apart from a few such limitations, one is left with every possible opportunity to produce interesting, original and lively work.

46   *Bag   Joan Spinney, aged 16/17, Bromley Grammar School*

Two examples with an unusual touch are of bags by pupils, aged 16/17, from Bromley Grammar School. They each show a band of canvas work applied to a linen ground. In the first, two rich bands of other forms of stitchery are worked using the same warm browns and oranges as in the central area, thus giving the necessary support and finish to what would otherwise be a rather stark application. The second is in cool green and cream wools and other threads, and once again the accompanying bands of other forms of stitchery give a subtlety of division to the whole shape.

45   *Bag   Gillian Richardson, aged 16/17, Bromley Grammar School*

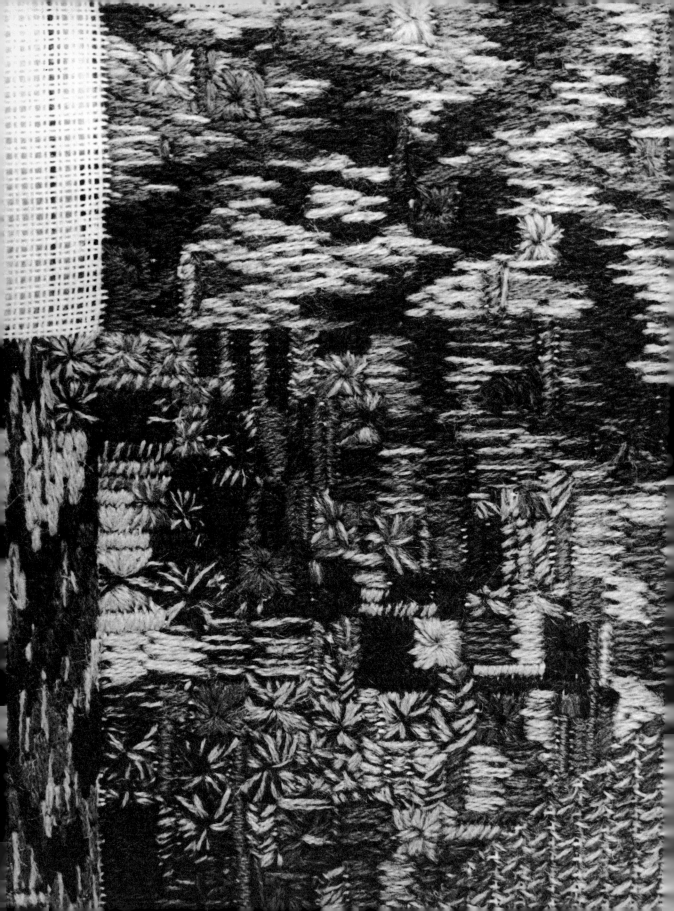

A partly finished stool top offers ideas for the inclusion of unusual threads such as raffine. It is worked entirely in black and white, with the black ground being of particular interest due to the way in which the stitch is altered in size and thickness giving a most interesting relief without any of the complications that would result from introducing stitches that are not of the same character as the basic ground.

50   Stool top   *Gillian Parker, Avery Hill College of Education*

◀ 49   Detail of sample area   *Maureen Ellis, Avery Hill College of Education*

In complete contrast to the last example, in which the approach was meticulous as well as original, is a detail of embroidery that suggests uses such as a pulpit fall. Here is an extremely free yet practical texture worked in light and dark blues. This treatment results in the creation of a lively surface.

Triangular experiments could also provide valuable thoughts on pulpit falls. The above *Burning Bush* panel is worked in flame stitch, using raffia, floss silk and wool. The colours are from black, through blue to orange, reds and pinks.

47   *Burning Bush   Lorna Derbyshire*

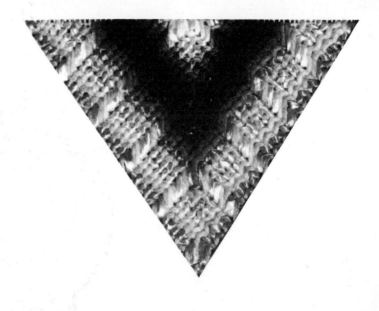

48a, b   Samplers   *Lorna Derbyshire*

71

Two further stool tops are of special interest. The first is a detail and the second is a complete work, but both show different bold divisions of area with particular emphasis on the horizontal and vertical lines of back stitching between the lines of gobelin.

52   Stool top   *Dorothy Cash, Avery Hill College of Education*

◀ 51   Detail of stool top   *Florence Baker,*
Avery Hill College of Education

A circular stool cushion in brilliant yellows, oranges and reds with some warm but dull greens has been worked in a variety of stitches and threads. The petals of the design of a flower have been carefully placed so as to leave a series of related shapes between them. They are worked in knitting stitch to add to the feeling of direction and growth, thereby introducing an impression of movement within a fairly static pattern. The centre is built up richly with spots and clusters of velvet stitch, gobelin and knotted. The gussets are not in canvas work and (as they are not seen when the cushion is sunk into the stool top) have instead been made in heavy pure linen of a matching colour.

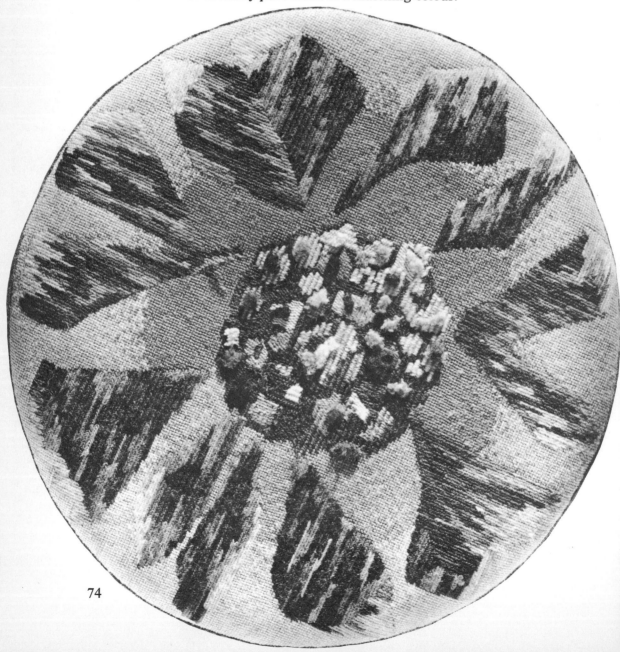

In another cushion, of which a detail is shown, an evenweave linen has been substituted for canvas, but a free adaptation of rococo stitch has been used. In this way it has been possible to employ canvas work stitches without the necessity of covering an entire background.

54 Detail of linen cushion cover   *Dorothy Gutteridge, Maidstone College of Art*

53 Circular stool stop   *Marjorie Cox, Maidstone College of Art*

Canvas embroidery has often been linked with ecclesiastical work and today many projects for kneelers and cushions are carried out in this way. A few examples dealing with this field of work may therefore be of interest and help.

A very large scheme of 42 kneelers and 42 stall cushions is at present being organised by Lady Younger for Iona Abbey. Their designer is Adam Robson, whose project is exacting in that half the cushion designs are Coats of Arms of the clans connected with Iona Abbey and the others are of the Four Evangelists, St Columbus's Last Words and verses from the *Benedicite*. The intricate subject matter evolves into simple areas of pattern as can be seen in the stall cushion illustrated. It is worked mainly in cross stitch with occasional use of rice and gobelin. It is therefore most valuable for the ideas it offers on the meticulous planning of the whole scheme of designs, the importance of the placing of each design within its total area and the careful distribution of the light and shade.

55   Iona Abbey stall cushion, Coat of Arms of the Duke of Argyll

While on the subject of schemes for kneelers, a word also about the planning of entire colour schemes should be mentioned. The colours for a scheme should be selected not only so that each cushion is beautiful, but so that each cushion is related also to the whole scheme and, most important of all, to the church as a whole. This total beauty of a large scheme is rarely found, but one example is to be seen in Coventry Cathedral. Here, in spite of the somewhat linear designs, the whole scheme is entirely appropriate to the cathedral. Six designs are repeated the required number of times. The colours are both brilliant and sombre and range from purples, mauves, purple pinks, red and black to greens, contributing in all a most moving complement to the entire brilliance of the interior of the cathedral.

A beautifully designed chair seat for the Airman's Chapel, South-well Minster, provides an example of the difficult task of combining totally different families of shapes. It is a complex design in that the two dominant sets of wings are of a different character of shape. However, the shape of the space between each set of wings has much in common and the fact that light areas occur in both in the pleasing proportions of one-third in the lower set to two-thirds in the upper set certainly brings the design together. The area around them repeats the rhythms of the wings in the fine dark lines which in turn are reiterated in the total outline of the cushion itself. The whole is a completely compact and successful statement.

56 Chair seat for Airman's Chapel, Southwell Minster   *Anne Butler*

Another complex subject, that of the Arms of the Duchy of Lancaster, is beautifully treated in the sanctuary chair cushion for Langham Church. A beautiful sense of pattern links one shape to another and to the shield itself. The whole is set on a rich and original texture using rice and straight gobelin.

57 Sanctuary chair cushion for Langham Church *Kathleen Carless*

Large scale schemes for kneelers are common. Some of the best and most interesting undoubtedly occur when the entire scheme is designed in the main by one artist, leaving only a little freedom to those actually carrying it out. Two such schemes are those for Lincoln Cathedral and Eton College, Cambridge, which were largely designed by Constance Howard. One of the exceptions to the scheme at Eton are the substall cushions of the Evangelists by Elizabeth Willink (59). Rich, panel-like areas contrast with plain expanses to become part of the happy division of the rectangular cushion.

The design for the other kneeler shown here is by Constance Howard. The scheme is based on the subject of Mary Magdalene and here the pattern is derived from the flowing strands of her hair. Note the unusual link of the top with the gussets.

58   Kneeler, Lincoln Cathedral

Hanging by Leonore Prasa
See page 87

59   Sub-stall cushion, Eton College   *Elizabeth Willink*

Successful decoration, however, need not always depend on elaborate ingredients. Two stool tops for Loundsley Green Church reveal this. The accompanying illustration shows one of them. The dominant tone of the cross boldly divides the rectangle and within this seemingly simple main shape can be found great variation in texture of stitchery. A subtle presentation of the circle can just be detected behind the cross where the background tent stitch gives way to cross stitch.

60   Stool top, Loundsley Green Methodist Church   *Anne Butler*

A rich texture is beginning to emerge in the kneeler depicting the International Harvester's Emblem. Here it is possible to see the way in which the sheaves of wheat are prevented from being isolated by the rich textures occurring amidst the low relief of the tent stitch because of the similar textures in the surrounding shapes.

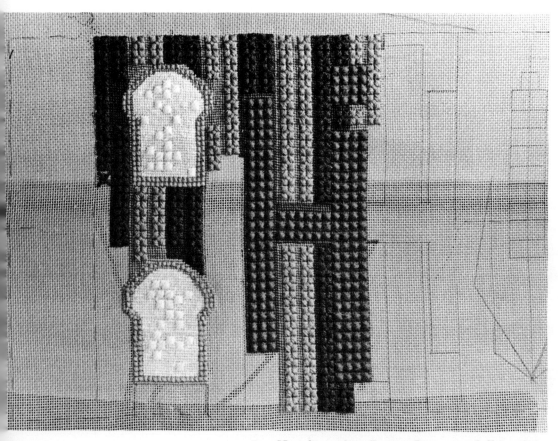

61   Kneeler   *Amy Brown, Doncaster College of Art*

A project with roots in the past was the re-covering of a mid-Victorian chair. The whole is a rich and beautifully designed project and, as can be seen from the accompanying photographs, has a wealth of texture. Crewel and rya rug wools have been used and in the depth of some of the stitches a few beads have been used. A convolvulus plant was the basis of the design and from this very accurate study of nature (see page 27) came this vigorous design in reds, pinks, purples and greens working out to the edges where a band of buffs, off-whites and silvers has a beauty all of its own.

Overleaf

62   Completed embroidery for mid-Victorian prie-dieu or Pusey chair
     Annette Firth

63   Detail   83

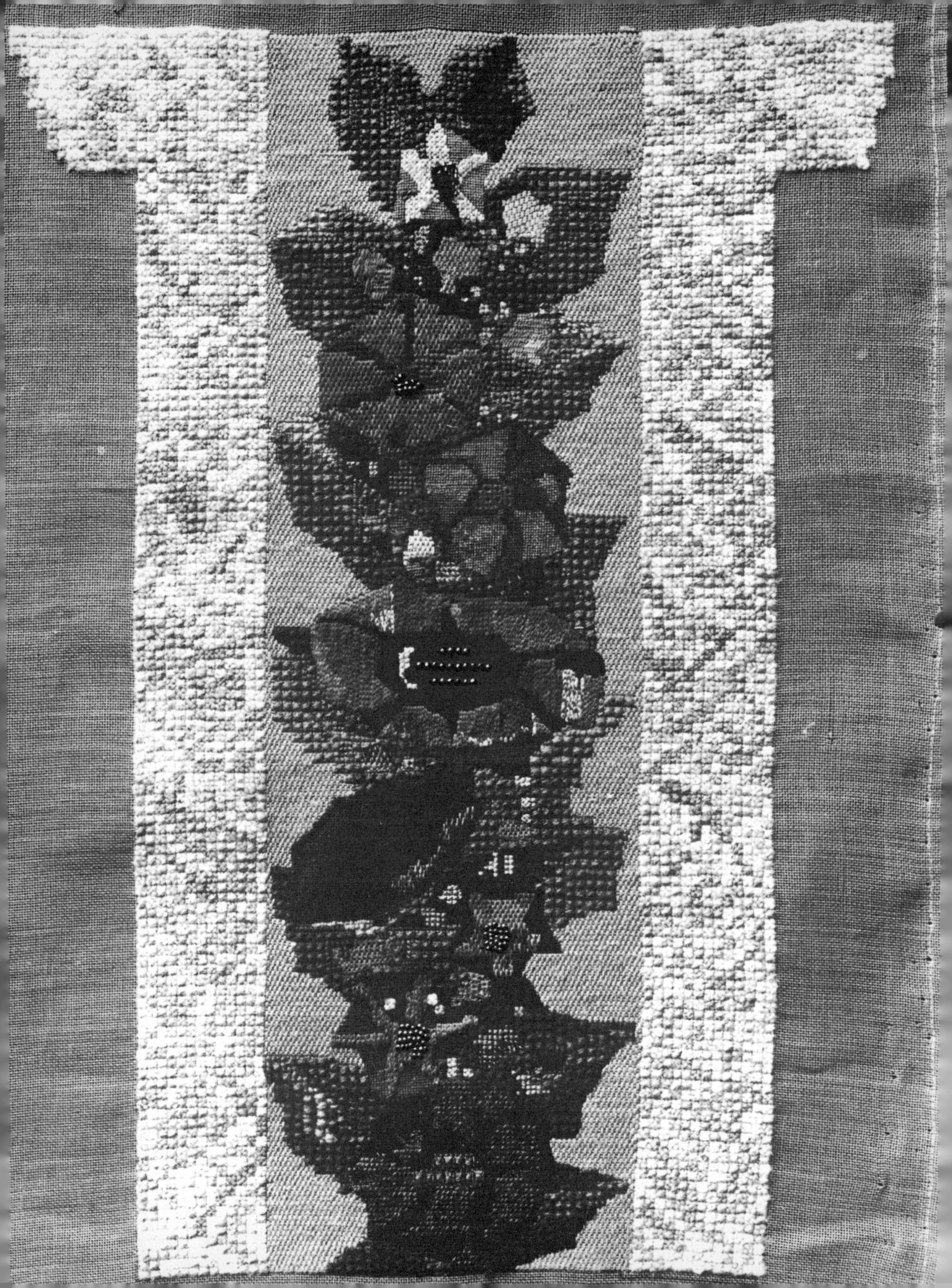

As a final note to this group of works, the next photograph is offered to suggest a new starting point for a kneeler. Hard-wearing canvas work stitches have been set into a leather surround. There are so many leather fabrics on the market which would wear well and could cut the cost and labour in certain schemes where this is a major consideration. The canvas has been continued behind the leather, but care should be taken in selecting a leather or leather fabric of a strong enough quality to wear well and not show the texture of the lines of the canvas beneath.

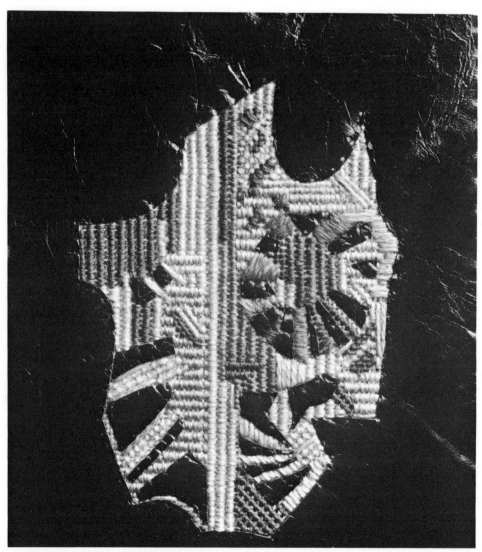

64 Experiment for a kneeler *Diana Springall*

Experiments in the use of stitchery for decorative purposes, and practical only in the sense that they serve to decorate a wall

Although, however, these are for convenience dealt with separately here they should not be entirely isolated from the preceding section, for they still form very much a part of the total aim—that of furthering and widening the possibilities of the medium in every way.

One project that may admirably form a link between the practical and the purely decorative is the carpet hanging design by the Porguguese artist Leonore Prasa where an average canvas has been used in such a way that it would be as successful for the floor as for the wall. See colour plate opposite page 81.

Original techniques and approaches that lend themselves admirably to large scale wall decoration are amongst the first suggestions and examples. Up to this point in the book, traditional canvas has been used throughout for the ground fabric or basic structure. However, there is no need to limit oneself to canvas; one can, for example, carry out certain experiments using hand-built wire grids as shown in the following three illustrations. The first two are executed in coarse string. The first offers ample scope for ideas for a large open screen either allowing the passage of light to flow through or to be set against a colour or colours of great intensity. The second could also be on a large scale if desired and could be used to texture a wall of any length. They are both in fact details from a three-dimensional form which in turn leads one to yet another set of thoughts, including possible uses in the sphere of sculptural interpretations.

Overleaf
65–66   Details of three-dimensional form in string   *Heather Barnard*

The third example is on a grid of a less regular nature than the first two, and is worked in a variety of brightly coloured wools together with japanese gold thread. This too offers scope for more than surface decoration; it could, for example, be used for open screens and room divisions of various sorts in almost any scale.

67 Panel *Diana Bates, Goldsmiths' College School of Art*

There are also many metal grids that, unlike the last, are machine-made and the following three examples are simple uses of chicken wire. These, like the previous three, lend themselves to all kinds of possibilities as decoration of vertical surfaces, but also, in the case of 69 and 70, offer scope, by reason of the extreme sparseness of the wools used, for subtle and exciting uses in conjunction with artificial lighting for such things as suspended or false ceilings or screens.

In the example below of this group, one can easily detect not only simple canvas work stitches but their combination with such things as needle weaving and raised chain band.

68–70 Experiments using chicken wire *Diana Bates, Goldsmiths' College School of Art*

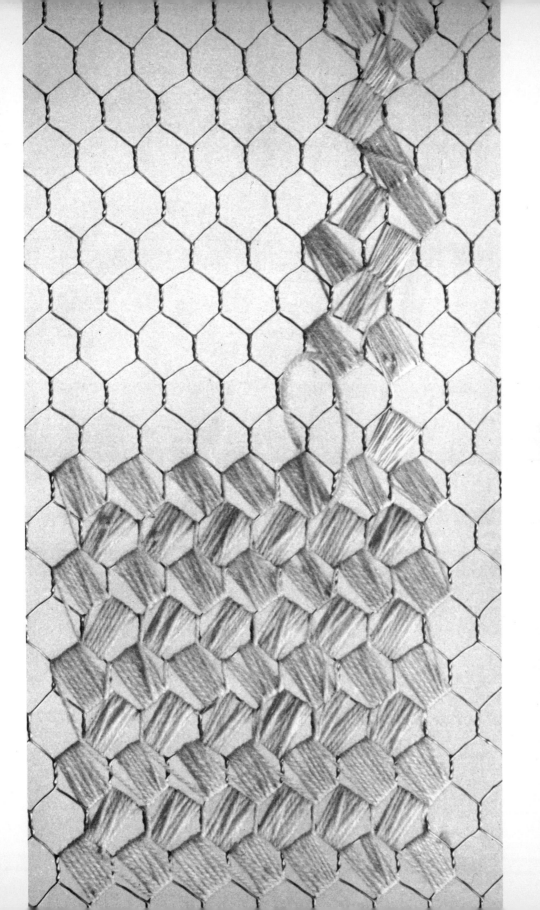

Two prolific artists whose main work involves the execution of large-scale wall decorations in this form of embroidery are, firstly, the Belgian artist Corine Toussein and, secondly, the South African, Miriam Sacks.

The first two photographs show beautiful examples worked in knotted stitch on turkey carpet canvas. The first, which is entitled *Body and Soul* and measures 7 feet square, has been worked entirely in white. The second, *Temps Gris*, is 9 feet by 7 feet and is derived from sea artemones and marine fauna and worked in greens and greys. In both of them the subtle low relief is a source of pleasure and it will also be observed that in both the entire canvas has been closely

71 *Body and Soul   Corine Toussein*

covered. In the case of the work of Miriam Sacks, however, also working in similarly large dimensions, a much freer attack is made on the canvas. The *Machine Men* which has been executed with a degree of boldness amounting almost to brutality, gives an impression of what one might describe as a spontaneous approach; study of the detail photograph clearly shows, for example, how part of the canvas has been intentionally left exposed and reveals also the impulsive free nature of the wool and lurex stitchery.

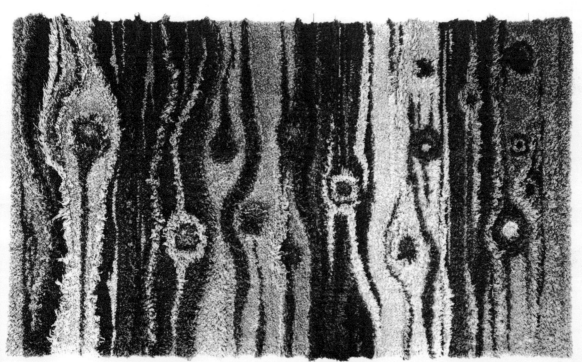

72   *Temps Gris   Corine Toussein*

73   *Machine Men Miriam Sacks*

73a Detail of *Machine Men Miriam Sacks* ▶

The combination of fabric appliqué and canvas work also occurs in another large work where fabric strips are used in lieu of wool or other threads. Florentine stitch is chiefly used except in the halo around the sun where the strips of fabric have been threaded through from the back, between the two areas of checked and striped fabrics, giving a texture similar to a rag rug.

The following two illustrations both represent work that could be undertaken on a large scale, although could equally well succeed if a miniature translation were required. In fact the huge double cross stitches of the first example, executed in thick wool on a large canvas, were done on a big scale and could well be used to provide some form of optical illusion or recession, either in this or some equally dominant pattern.

The second is particularly interesting by reason of its very skilful connection of applied fabric with the rest of the panel. The stripes of the applied fabrics not only repeat the stripes of the large areas of laid threads but of the two areas of close stitchery. The stitching on the top right side closely resembles darning and is divided by a narrow braid, whereas the lower patch of stitching is a completely original division of cross stitch stripes by a line of couching combined with back stitch. The laid threads are safely secured by ironing the canvas work on the wrong side because the glue from the canvas provides right qualities of adhesion.

◀ 74 *Evening Sun* 5-foot panel *Eirian Short*

79 Panel *Masie Green, Doncaster College of Art*

The meticulous weaving stitches of the last work leads one to the freer interpretations of a similar theme. The woven thread in the detail of a piece by Linda Knight shows the use of thick wool combined with portions of already woven fabric to give a rich surface completely covering the canvas.

These ideas are, as one can see, used in an even freer way in the above photograph, where the bamboo strips completely alter the character of the basic canvas and this pleasing result helps to make one realise that there is a wealth of possibilities to be explored in combining the use of other materials with canvas.

On a large rug canvas this has been carried even further by the use, in lieu of thread, of strips of cloth which have been combined with various *objets trouvés*.

103

The next group of five works all depend on traditional stitchery, but have been grouped together to show the great difference in techniques when several people set out merely to enjoy and expand the possibilities of canvas work.

The first illustration has been selected for the lightness of quality, the variety of stitch and texture and the pleasant use made of the exposed canvas threads.

82 Panel *Olive Cocker, Doncaster College of Art*

A similar freedom is also evident in the next two illustrations. The first, *Bird with Flowers*, is worked in raffia and wool, with beads and felt applied and the second is a design based on an African head, worked in raffia and wool.

80 *Bird with Flowers   Linda Beard, Liverpool Regional College of Art* ▶

81 Design based on African head
Ruth McCulloch, Liverpool Regional College of Art

The two details of panels that follow are rich in the variety of threads used—velvet, ribbons, cord, raffene, many wools and chenille. Each small portion of these details also suggests a wide range of exciting possibilities for exploration in the fascinating realm that this field of embroidery offers. The first shows the actual canvas bound with raffene reminiscent of a Mexican sampler of 1867 in the Victoria and Albert Museum, London.

83   Panel   *Vina Saville, Stockwell College of Education*

84 Panel *Peggy George, Stockwell College of Education*

Part II   Stitches

The purpose of this section is to save the embroiderer time in two important ways. Firstly, to display at a glance the working of every known stitch. Secondly, to show the texture produced by that stitch when it is reproduced in quantity, thus alleviating the need, in most cases, to make laborious test samples before commencing work. The complete information about each stitch appears on one page and the photographs in each case have been enlarged four times.

For simplification and easy comparison, the stitch samples have all been worked on the same size of canvas, 18 holes to the inch, with the exception of rep stitch which demands a double canvas (see section on types of canvas). There are three other stitches, half cross, knitting and web, which are also normally worked on a double canvas but, as can be seen, work equally well on a single mesh. With web stitch, however, when working on a single mesh canvas, a better result is achieved by starting each new line two rows down instead of one.

Crewel wool of a double thickness has been used in most of the illustrations. In some cases, however, the nature of the stitch requires a variation; for example, some stitches worked in two thicknesses would not satisfactorily cover the canvas and others would overcrowd the canvas if the thickness were not reduced to half. However, varying the number of threads does not alter the main structure of the texture. The stitches which require a variation of thickness are plaited, algerian, single knotted and web which have been worked in four thicknesses, and chain, cross, half cross, french, plaited and eastern which are all worked in a single thickness. The other exceptions to the use of crewel wool of double thickness are to be found in reversed cross, which is worked in one thickness of wool together with one strand of silk; rice, which is in two strands of wool with the light tone in one strand of silk; and rococo, which is in one strand of silk.

For simplification the wool throughout is in one tone with the exception of reversed cross, rice and florentine in which a second tone has been used to provide greater clarity. Naturally most stitches can be worked to advantage in more than one tone. One example can be seen in illustration 122 where parisian is worked in several tonal combinations.

List of Stitches

110

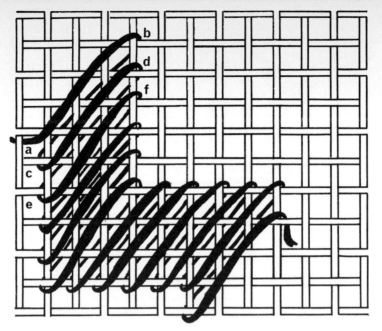

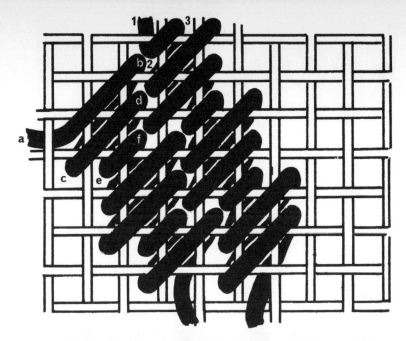

87 Cashmere

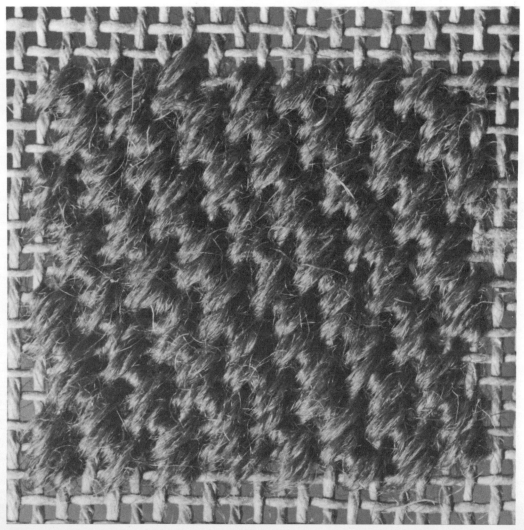

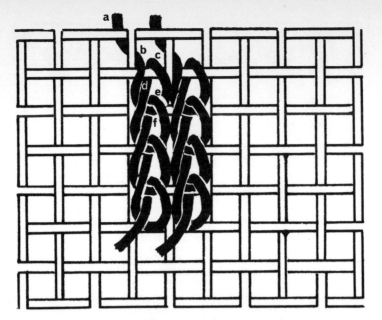

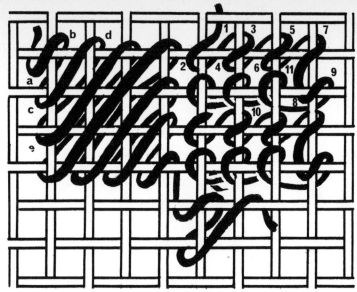

89 Chequer

Repeat in alternate blocks

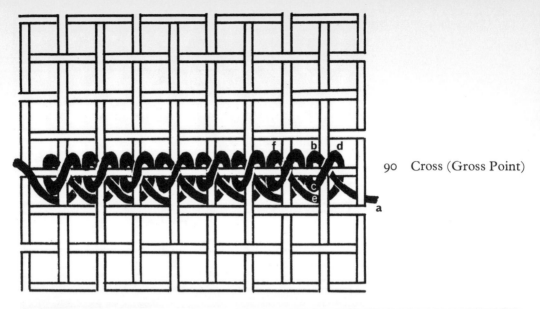

90 Cross (Gross Point)

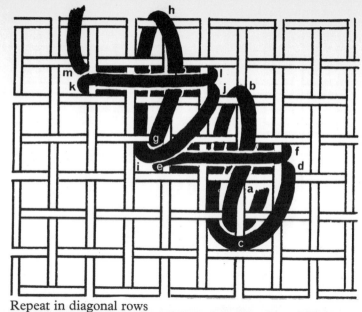

91　Cross, Diagonal

Repeat in diagonal rows

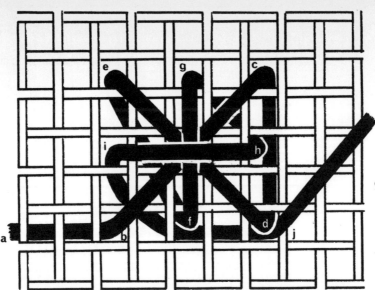

92 Cross, Double
(Leviathan or Smyrna)

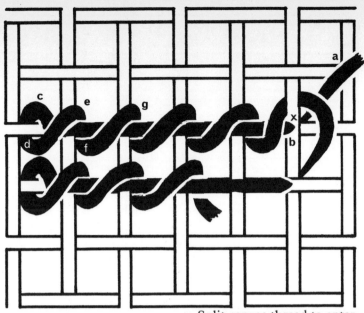

93   Cross, Half

x Split canvas thread to enter

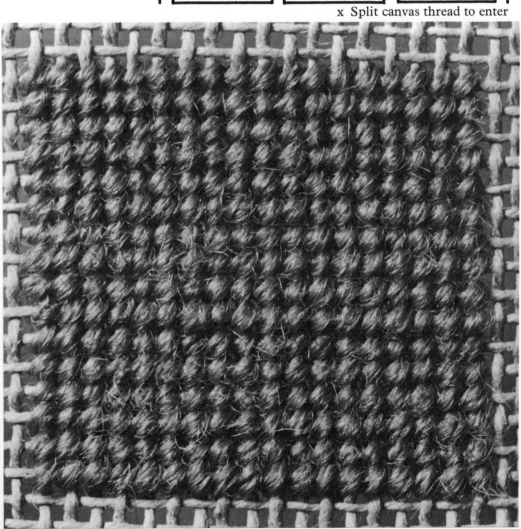

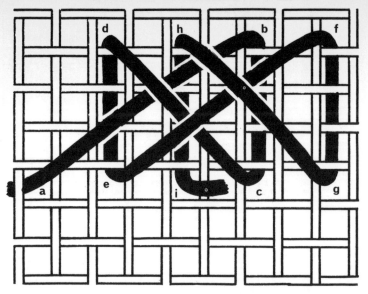

94   Cross, Long-armed

95 Cross, Montenegrin

Repeat as (a) (b)

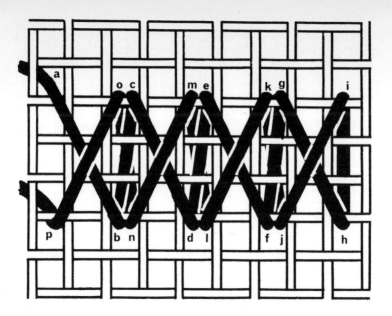

96 Cross, Oblong

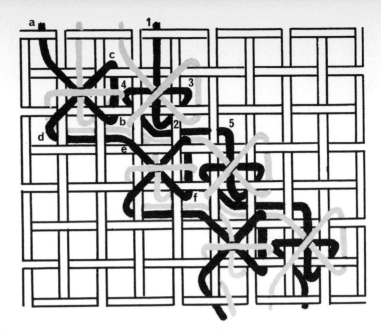

97   Cross, Reversed

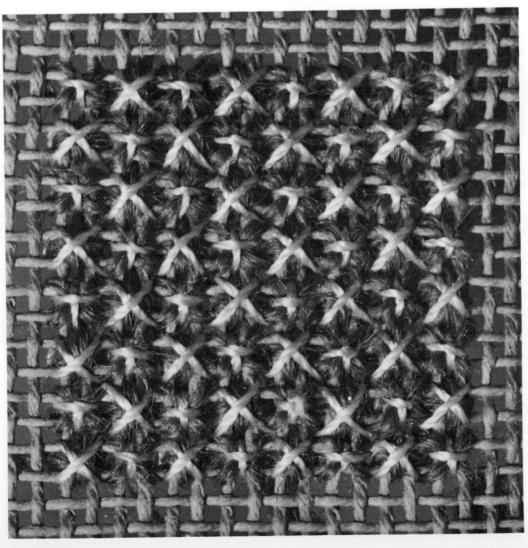

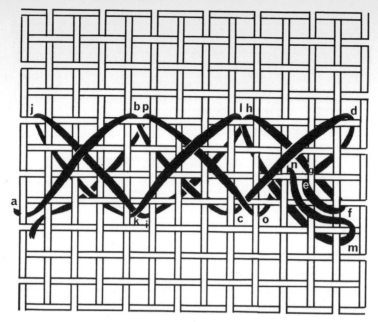

98 Cross, Two-sided

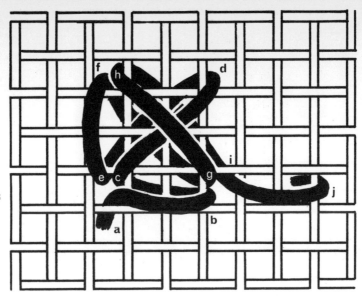

99 Cross, Italian
(Two-sided Italian Cross
or Arrowhead Cross)

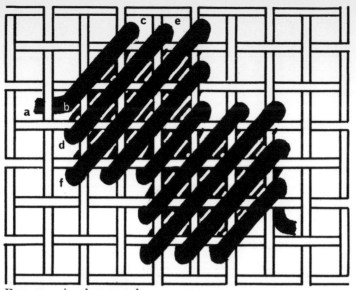

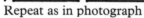

Repeat as in photograph

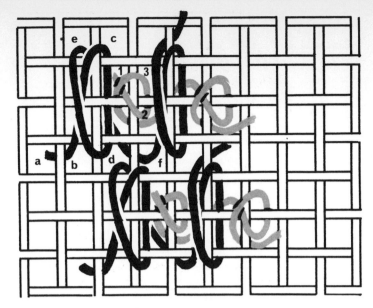

101 Double

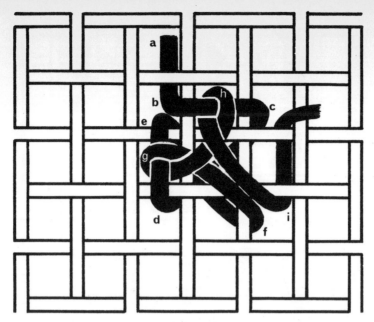

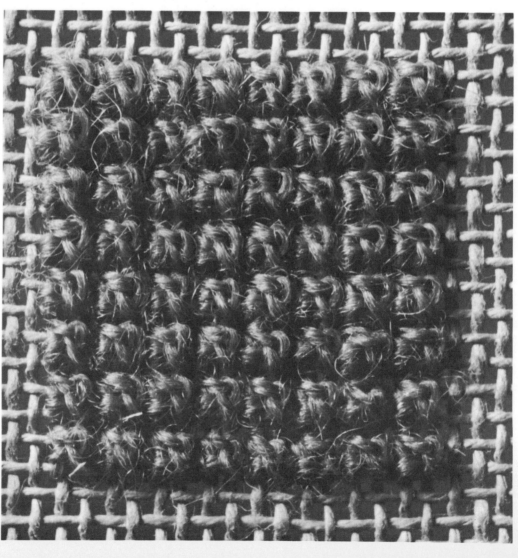

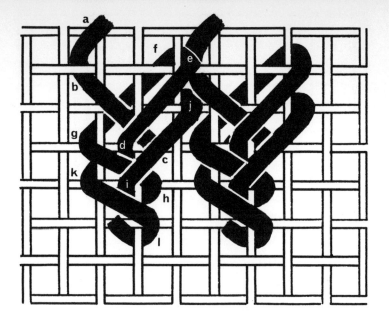

103 Fern

104 Fishbone

Repeat row is worked upside down

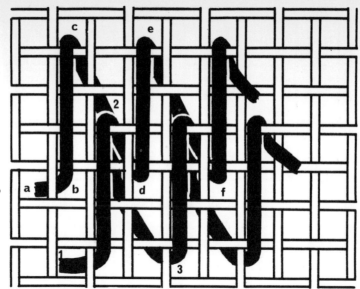

105   Florentine (Cushion,
      Flame or Irish)

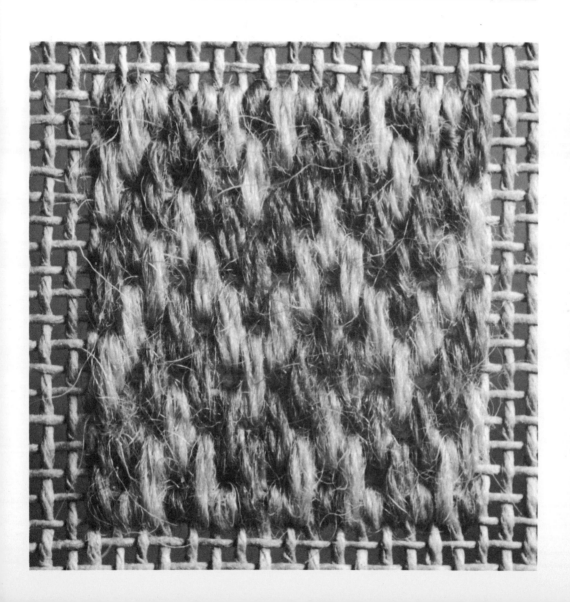

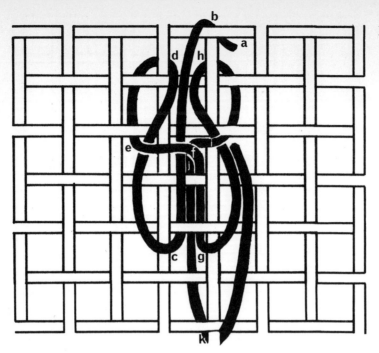

Repeat in vertical rows
(k) is position for start of
next stitch as (d) (e), and
so on

106   French

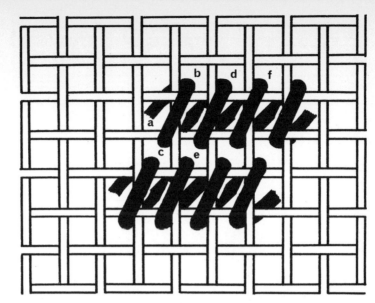

107 Gobelin
(Oblique Gobelin)

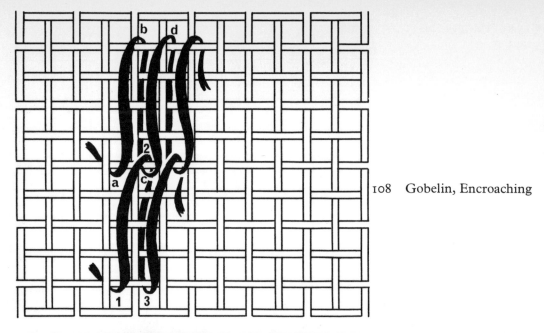

108   Gobelin, Encroaching

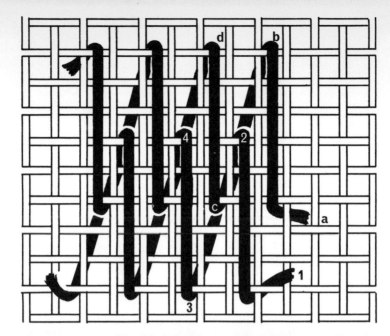

109 Gobelin, Filling

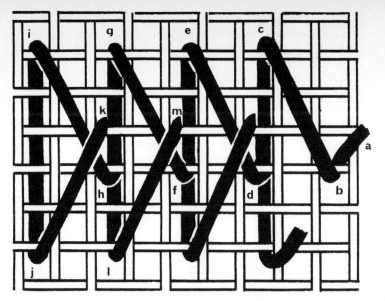

110　Gobelin, Plaited

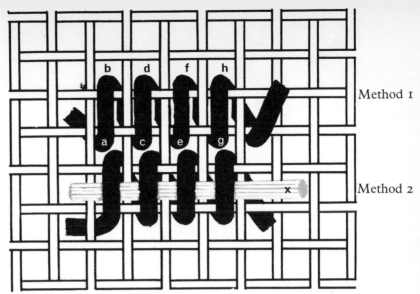

Method 1

Method 2

111 Gobelin, Straight
(Upright Gobelin)

x Laid thread

112   Gobelin, Wide

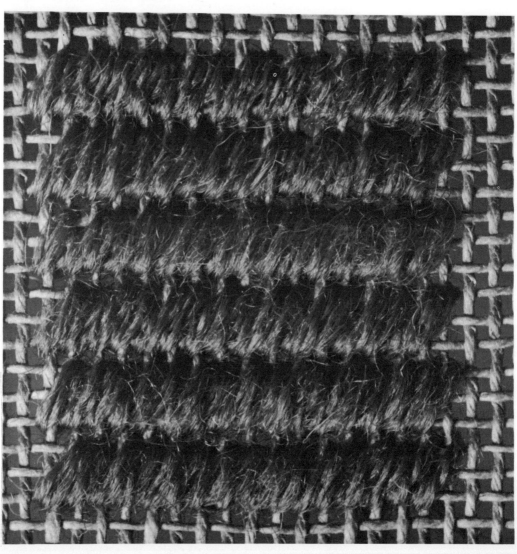

Note second row is worked upside down

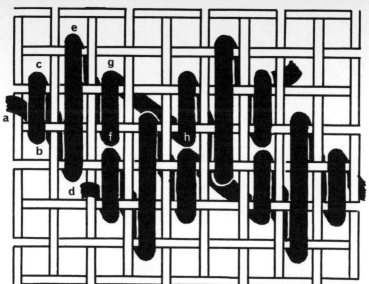

114 Hungarian (Mosaic when worked diagonally)

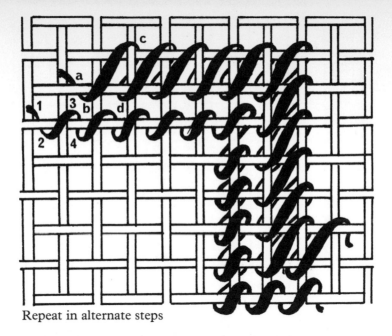

Repeat in alternate steps

115   Jacquard

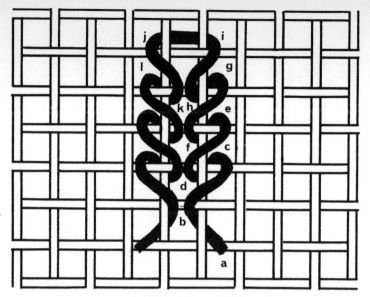

116 Knitting (Tapestry)

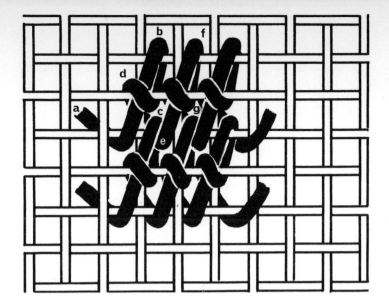

117 Knotted

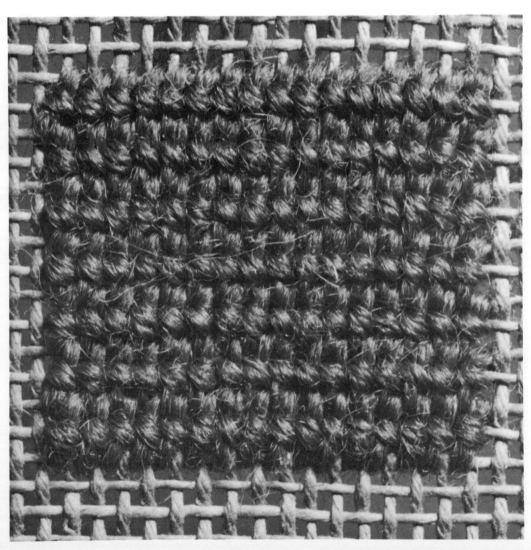

Trim ends afterwards

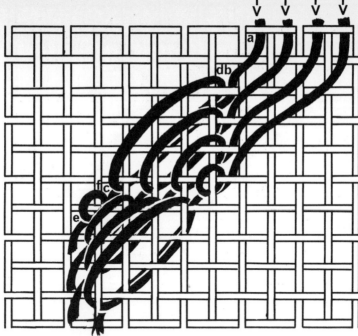

Four rows of diagonal back stitch forms each pattern

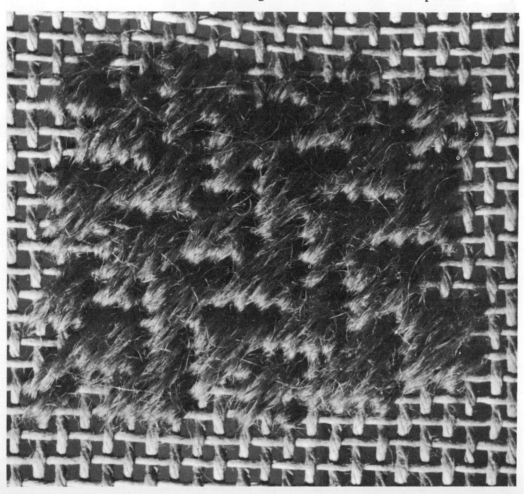

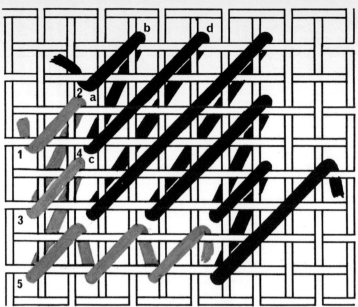

The new position for the repeat of point (a) will be the twelfth hole to the right or left, excluding the one in which point (a) occurs

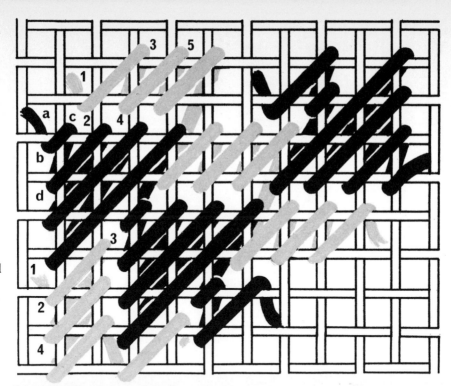

Note repeats of grey thread are in steps of three; horizontal blocks in one row and vertical in the next

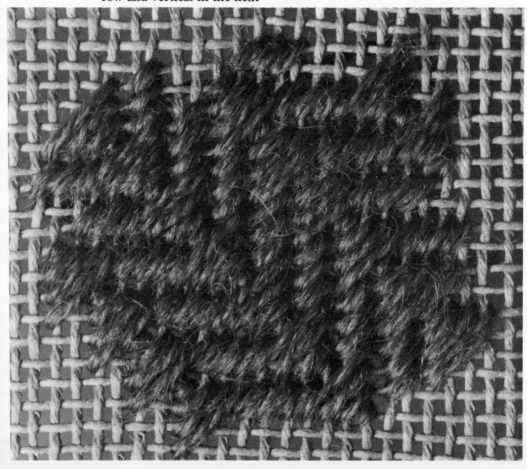

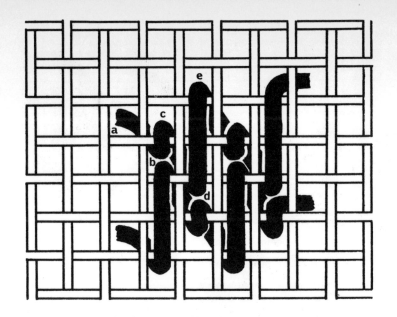

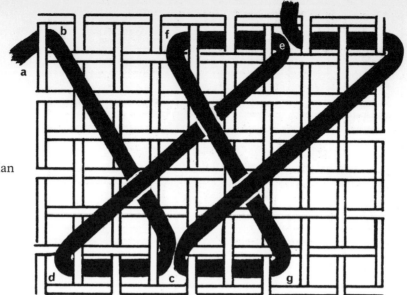

123 Plaited Algerian

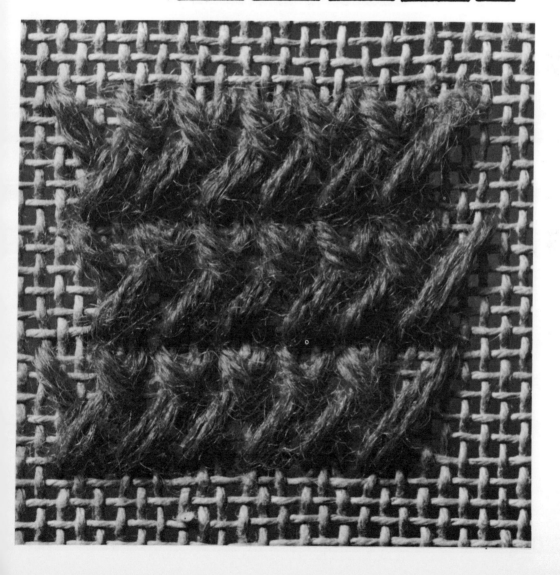

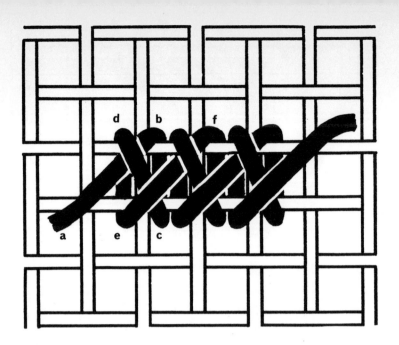

d　b　f

a　e　c

124　Plait (Spanish)

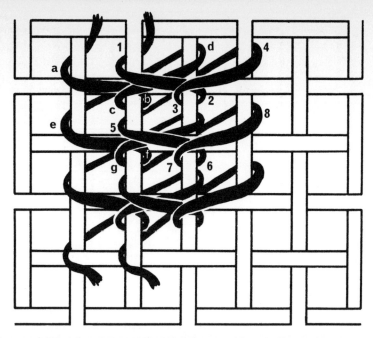

125 Plaited

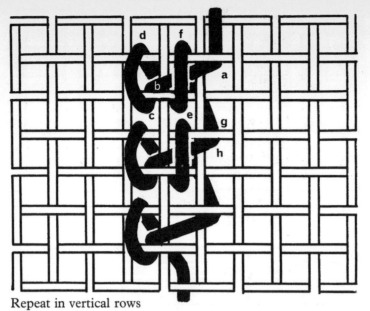

Repeat in vertical rows

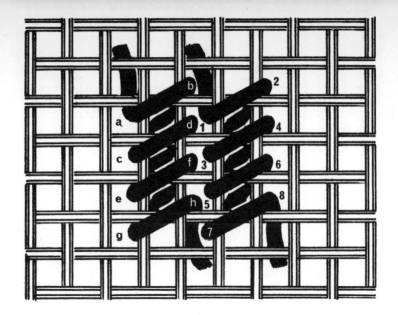

127   Rep (Aubusson)

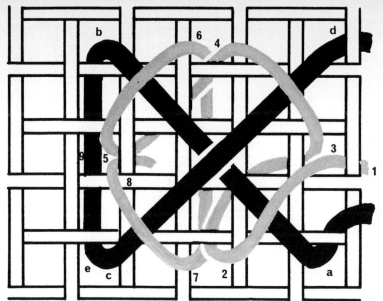

Repeat of black thread starts at point (e),
and repeat of grey thread at point 9

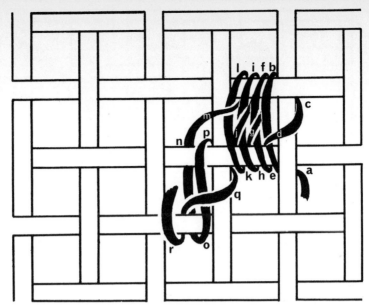

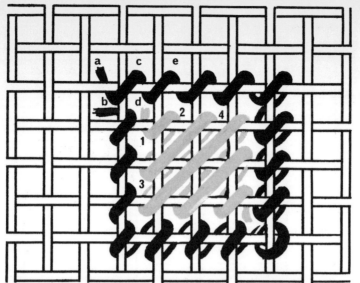

Repeat as in photograph

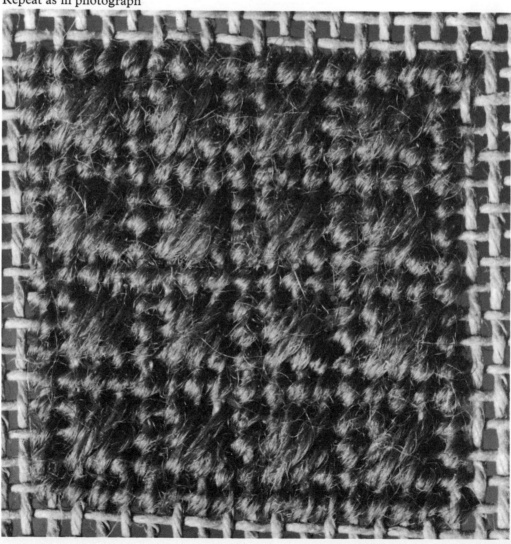

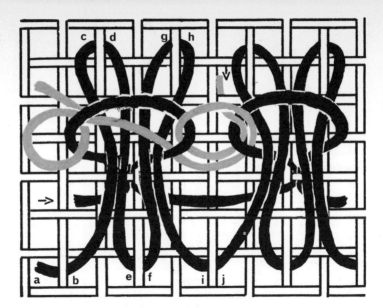

1 Work from (a)
2 Work from arrow at left
3 Grey line

131 Shell

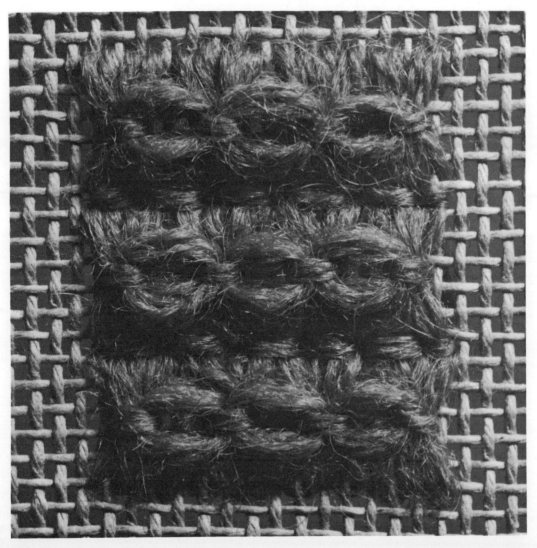

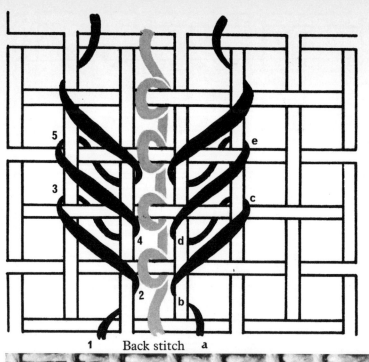

5

3

4   d

e

c

2   b

1   Back stitch   a

132   Stem

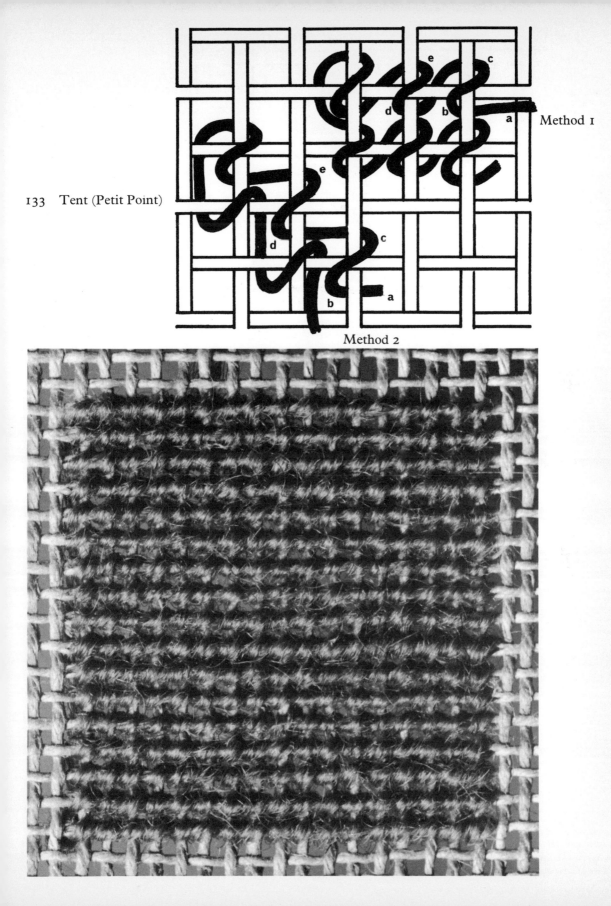

133   Tent (Petit Point)

Method 1

Method 2

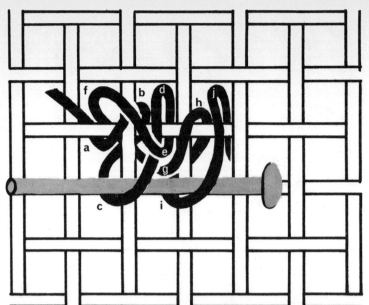

Knitting needle to hold loops fill end of row   Cut loops

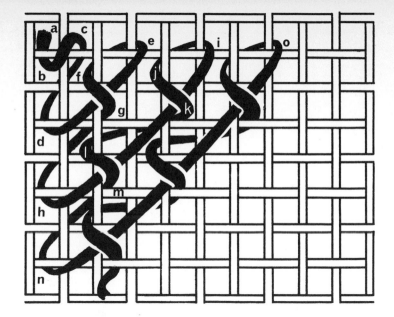

Part III Preparation and finish of work

How to enlarge or reduce a design

The size of the original design is often not the one required for the final work and the instructions and diagram will show clearly the simplest method of making it larger or smaller with great accuracy.

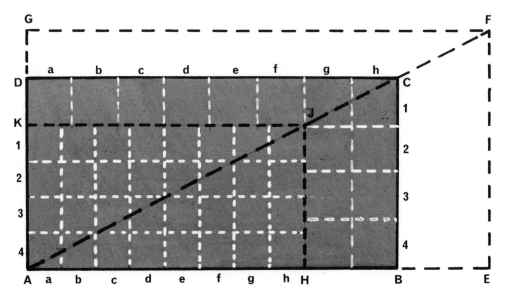

136   How to enlarge and reduce a design

1   Draw the area of the original design A, B, C, D on a piece of paper.
2   Join AC to form the diagonal.
3   *To enlarge*, extend AC to any point.
4   Decide on the new length of one of the sides, say AE, and extend to that point.
5   Erect a perpendicular from E to meet the extended diagonal at point F.
6   Extend AD to point G to make it the same length as EF.
7   Join FG.

8   The rectangle AEFG is now the new enlarged area proportionate to the original.

9   *To reduce*, decide on the desired length of one of the sides, say AH.

10 Erect a perpendicular from H to point J on the diagonal.

11 Mark off on AD the length of AK to equal HJ.

12 Join JK.

13 AHJK is now the desired reduced area, proportionate to the original.

14 Whether enlarging or reducing, divide the original design area ABCD into a number of equal squares. When a design is not intricate or is large, these squares could be 2 or 3 inches. Small or intricate work requires smaller divisions.

15 Let us say that side AB is 4 inches divided into eight $\frac{1}{2}$-inch squares.

The new area, whether larger or smaller, must be divided into the same number of divisions. So, if AB is reduced to AH measuring, say, 3 inches, each division will be $\frac{3}{8}$-inch square. In this way, whatever part of the design occurs in a certain square of the original area can be accurately assessed and transferred to the new dimensions.

16 The squares on both should be identically numbered and lettered for easy reference.

To prepare for work

Having got the design to the required size

1   Ink or blacken the lines of the design.

2   Lay canvas over design.

3   With a fine paint brush and black waterproof ink transfer the lines of the design on to the canvas. Black is usually used, but if the work is to be executed in pale colours, it is advisable to use ink of a lighter colour.

Frames

The type necessary for this kind of work are called slate frames and vary slightly according to the manufacturer. The most common are as in the diagram. Suppliers are listed on page 177.

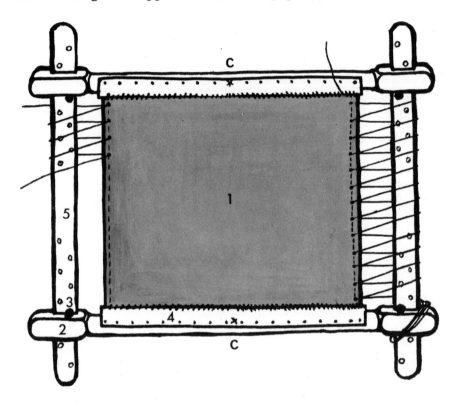

137 Slate frame

C: Centre
1 Canvas
2 Rollers
3 Pegs at each corner
4 Webbing
5 Slats or battens

How to dress a frame

Essential procedure for this type of work. It ensures that the canvas cannot become distorted during work and enables the embroidress to work evenly with both hands
1   Cut the canvas along the grain to about 2 inches larger than the area required for the design.
2   Bind the edges securely with bias tape of not less than 2 inches width to reinforce and prevent fraying. The grain should once again be carefully followed. If desired the two selvedge edges can be turned once and stitched over an insertion of fine string for extra strength.
3   Lay each roller (with webbing attached) in a horizontal position.
4   Mark the centre of webbing on each.
5   Attach the centre of the non-selvedge edge of the canvas with a pin to the centre of the webbing.
6   Stitch firmly to the webbing working from centre outwards, in either herringbone or overcast stitches.
7   Do the same with the opposite side of the canvas and second roller.
8   If length of work is longer than the length of the slats, roll surplus over rollers.
9   Place slats or batons through holes and push apart as tightly as possible and drop pegs in.
10   Using a packing needle, lace the selvedge edges with fine string over the slats.

Stretching

Essential for perfectly finished results

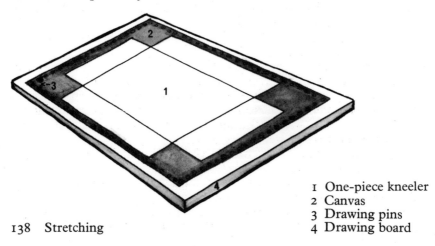

138   Stretching

1 One-piece kneeler
2 Canvas
3 Drawing pins
4 Drawing board

1   Lay several layers of blotting paper on a drawing board or old wooden surface.
2   Thoroughly wet the blotting paper.
3   Lay work face upwards on it.
4   With stout drawing pins carefully pin here and there on one edge making sure the grain is straight.
5   Pull the opposite side hard to achieve absolute tightness and insert several pins along the edge.
6   Treat the other two sides in the same way.
7   Continue to add further pins all round, pulling all the time, until they are about 1 inch apart and no wrinkles are left.
8   Allow to dry in a warm place overnight before removing pins.

Making up
A *Panels*
Canvas work, as can be seen from the chapters of both historical and contemporary embroidery, has many utilitarian functions, most of which require some making up. The following groups of instructions cover the most typical uses
Method 1   If the dimension of the panel is Imperial (22 inches by 32 inches) or less, the work can be placed over stout board. The work must be folded at least an inch over the edges of the board. These edges of the fabric must now be laced with fine string to the edges of the opposite side. The work should be quite taut on the right side.
Method 2   If the work is larger than Imperial board, wooden laths or batons are used. Once again the fabric is secured on the back but this time it is done with staples, tacks, etc., into the lath.

B Hangings

These can be made up a simple rectangle or can have numerous loops or sleeves for hanging, which allows the supporting baton to show.

After stretching, take a line around the outside shape. The work should then be laid face downwards on the table. A fairly heavy vilene or interlining such as dowlais, tailors' canvas, or unbleached calico, is cut almost to the finished size.

The edges of the work are then turned over, snipping corners and curves, on to the vilene and are then carefully herringbone stitched. The lining is cut with $\frac{1}{2}$-inch turnings, then slip-stitched on by hand still keeping the work flat on the table.

The sleeves if required are made in the same way as the main body of the banner and are laid in position one at each end and the rest at equal distances apart.

They are then stitched to the vilene and the top edge before the lining is applied and in turn stitched to them. The lining, when in place, should be a little inside the edge and slip stitching can commence after a centre tack line on both the back of the hanging and the lining are together.

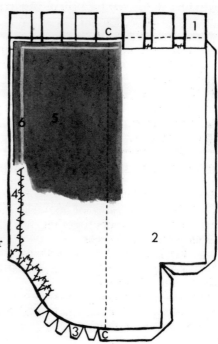

139　Making up a hanging

C: Centre
Centre lines of hanging
and lining must correspond
1 Sleeves
2 Interlining
3 Turnings before sewing
　showing snips for different
　shapes of edge
4 Turning sewn in position
5 Lining in finished position with
　turnings invisibly stitched under
6 White line denotes position of
　turned edge beneath lining

C *Kneelers*
Making up of a kneeler in one piece.
1 Cut out the kneeler leaving $\frac{3}{4}$ inch allowance for turnings.
2 Firmly stitch each corner so that, with the wrong side of the work uppermost, a shallow box is formed.
3 Lay a piece of carpet felt of the exact size of the top of the kneeler into the bottom of the box-shape.
4 Cut a piece of heavy duty foam to the dimensions of the kneeler (average size 9 inches by 12 inches by 2 inches deep). Layers of felt or similar material can be used instead. Pads of rubberised hair have also been found most satisfactory, keeping their shape well and being resilient yet firm. *The Hairlock Co. Ltd, Magna Works, Kathie Road, Bedford,* supply these to customers' requirements in minimum quantities of twenty-five. Two types are available, samples of which can be seen at the Embroiderers' Guild Headquarters, 73 Wimpole Street, London, W.1.
5 Cover the foam with hessian as one would do a neat parcel and stitch where necessary.
6 If the kneeler is to hang, the metal loop or curtain ring should be attached to three or four lengths of strong tape which in turn are stitched to the wrong side of the hessian-covered foam cushion. The tapes should be spread out at equal distances from the central point, where the loop is situated.
7 This is then settled into the canvas work shell or box and cotton wool is forced into the remaining spaces at the corners to ensure a good shape.
8 Bend the $\frac{3}{4}$-inch turnings over and, using a packing needle, lace from side to side with fine string. If the filling selected is very soft the lacing is omitted and the turnings are turned in and lightly stitched to the interior.
9 A backing material such as upholsterers' linen is then cut with an allowance for turnings. Pin and hem near the edge of the canvas.

Making up a kneeler with separately made gussets
1 With right sides of material facing each other, back-stitch or machine the gussets together.
Open seams and press.
2 Match centres of gussets with centres of each side of the top, keeping right sides together and stitch.
Open out and press.
3 Proceed as from 3 above.
Kneelers can also be made without gussets, inserting if desired a piping for extra finish.

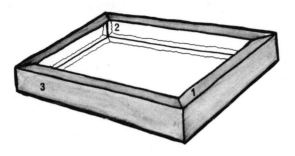

Kneeler face downwards
1 Turnings
2 Stitch corners to form box-shape
3 Gusset if applicable, otherwise sides of all-in-one shape

Hessian covered foam
Attach loop in centre with tapes for reinforcement

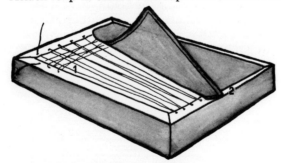

1 Lacing of turnings
2 Position of upholsterers' linen

140   Making up a kneeler

Part IV Materials

Canvas

The canvas which forms the ground fabric for the stitchery is obtainable in many types and sizes. It is, in fact, the canvas that gives the medium its unique character. A full selection is photographed here, actual size, to assist the beginner and the student to gain an understanding of what is offered. The widths of the various types and the character of each fabric are discernible at a glance, so that ordering by post is also possible. With this information the reader can link this section with other parts of the book and therefore have some idea what treatment various canvases will allow.

The main choice lies initially between a single or double canvas and, after that, it is mainly a case of choosing the canvas suited in size to the scale of the work to be done. It is safe to say that every stitch can be adapted to a single mesh canvas but this is not always the case with a double canvas, so, unless it is desired to undertake a particular experiment that requires a double canvas, the beginner will find single canvas a safer choice. The most useful size is 18 threads to the inch as it will take fine as well as coarser effects of stitchery, therefore allowing a variety of scale without altering the canvas.

The range of canvases available varies from place to place, but all the sizes listed here can be obtained from *Mace and Nairn, 89 Crane Street, Salisbury, Wiltshire.*

Colour also varies from supplier to supplier and it makes little difference which one is used. In any case the fine french canvas, i.e. 24, 28 and 32 threads to the inch, seems to be supplied in a variety of colour including off-white, pink and pale orange and certainly in this case the colour has no bearing on quality.

There are a few special canvases and other evenweave groundings which can form the basis for interesting experiment such as the flax canvas or jute embroidery cloth shown here or such types of evenweave woollen cloth where the thread is easily discernible.

12 threads per inch
Width 36 in., 90 cm   No. 12

14 threads per inch
Widths 26½, 36, 59 in., 65, 90, 150 cm   No. 14

16 threads per inch
Widths 26, 36, 59 in., 65, 90, 150 cm   No. 16

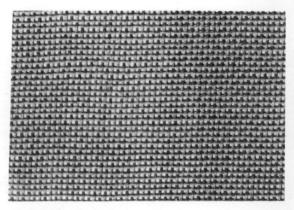

18 threads per inch
Width 36 in., 90 cm   No. 18
Also made in white, width 27 in., 68 cm

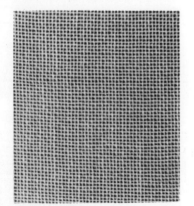

24 threads per inch
Width 24 in., 60 cm   No. 24

28 threads per inch
Width 24 in., 60 cm   No. 28

32 threads per inch
Width 24 in., 60 cm   No. 32

171

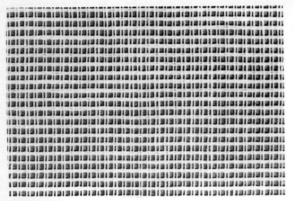

11 holes per inch
Width 24 in., 60 cm   No. 14 Penelope

12 holes per inch
Width 23 in., 59 cm   No. 24 Penelope

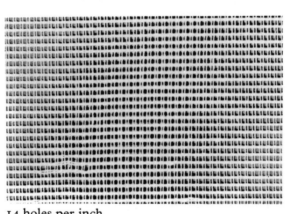

14 holes per inch
Width 25 in., 64 cm   No. 28 Penelope

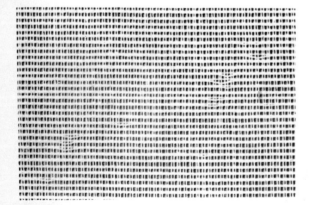

16 holes per inch
Width 25 in., 64 cm   No. 32 Penelope

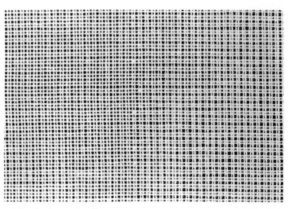

18 holes per inch
Width 25 in., 64 cm   No. 36 Penelope

Flax canvas in place of Winchester
17 threads per inch
Width 50 in., 127 cm

English canvas (white)
12 threads per inch   *Width* 27 in., 69 cm
Also made in 18 threads per inch

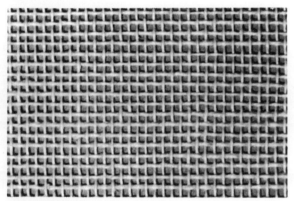

Raffia canvas
10 threads per inch
Widths 27, 18 in., 69, 46 cm

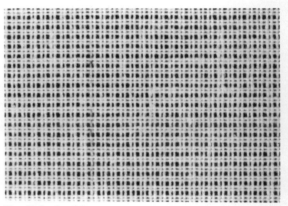

English double
10 holes per inch   *Widths* 19, 23 in.
48, 58 cm   No. 20 Penelope

Jute embroidery cloth
Widths 22, 27, 36, 48 in.
56, 69, 90, 120 cm

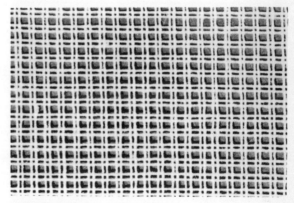

Danish white
7 holes per inch   *Width* 34 in.
86 cm   No. 14 Penelope

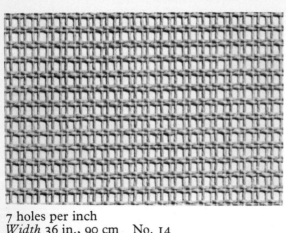

7 holes per inch
Width 36 in., 90 cm   No. 14

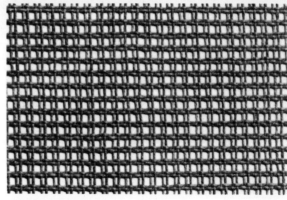

8 holes per inch
Width 36 in., 90 cm   No. 16

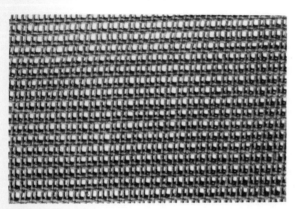

9 holes per inch
Width 36 in., 90 cm   No. 18

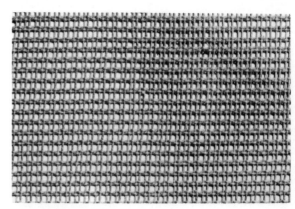

10 holes per inch
Widths 36, 26½ in., 90, 65 cm   No. 20

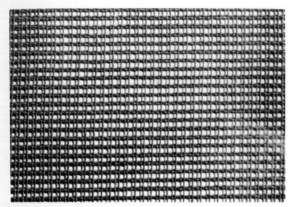

11 holes per inch
Widths 36, 26 in., 90, 65 cm   No. 22

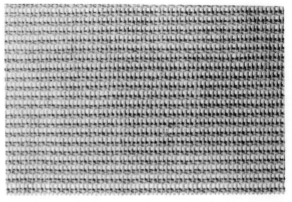

12 holes per inch
Widths 36, 26½ in., 90, 65 cm   No. 24

3 holes per inch
Widths 32, 40, 59 in., 81, 102, 150 cm

4 holes per inch
Widths 18, 27 in., 46, 69 cm

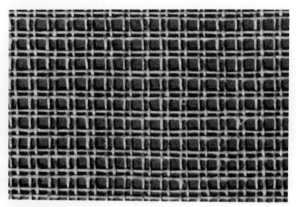

5 holes per inch
Widths 12, 18, 22, 27, 36 in.
30, 46, 56, 69, 90 cm

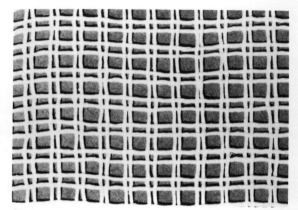

Smyrna
4 holes per inch
Width 39 in., 100 cm   No. 8 Penelope

Needles

Canvas work needles, or as the manufacturers call them, 'tapestry' needles, vary in size from 16 to 26 in the case of those made by Abel Morrall and 13 to 26 in the case of those made by Henry Milward. However, in both cases the sizes 19 to 26 correspond exactly to sizes 1 to 8 in an ordinary sewing needle. The actual sizes and character of these needles can be seen in the accompanying photograph. Their main feature is the blunt point to prevent severing the thread of the canvas. When selecting the correct needle for the canvas in hand, one must make sure that the needle will pass easily between the threads without 'expanding' them and should, thereafter, only have a large enough eye to carry the required thickness of wool or thread.

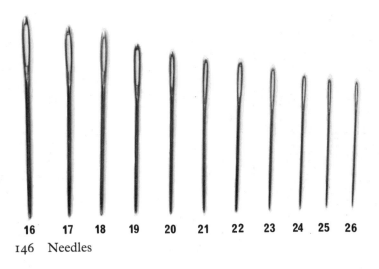

16 17 18 19 20 21 22 23 24 25 26

146 Needles

Thread

The main thread used on canvas, both in the past and at present, is wool. Crewel wool, which is made in the same range of colours as 'tapestry' wool, is by far the more hard wearing and pleasing to look at. It is certainly the most suitable for practical objects such as kneelers, stool tops, bags, etc., and can be happily combined with smaller quantities of other wools, stranded cotton, perlé, and coton à broder, to give variation and added excitement to the work.

Perlé is a shiny twisted thread where as coton à broder is a mat nonstranded thread. The best of these, together with stranded cotton are manufactured by D.M.C. and Cartier-Bresson and are distributed in Great Britain by *M.R. Ltd, 1a Thornford Road, Lewisham, London, S.E.13*, but can be bought from this address in quantity only. Small orders can be obtained from:

Mrs P. Coole, 12 Kingsley Avenue, Banstead, Surrey
Mace and Nairn, 89 Crane Street, Salisbury, Wiltshire
Mrs M. Allen, Turnditch, Derbyshire
Mrs I. M. Jervie, 21/23 West Port, Arbroath, Angus, Scotland
Royal School of Needlework, 25 Princes Gate, Kensington,
   London, S.W.7

These firms also meet overseas orders. The distributors in America are *The D.M.C. Corporation, 107 Trumbull Street, Elizabeth, New Jersey 07206*.

Rya rug wool is a hard-wearing twisted wool similar in character to crewel wool but a much larger scale and can be used in canvas work to advantage on sizes of 18 threads to the inch or larger. These and similar wools can be obtained from:

The Needlewoman Shop, Regent Street, London, W.1
Thomas Hunter, 36 Northumberland Street, Newcastle upon Tyne,
who also do a range of their own border wools.

Almost any thread can be used provided it is suitable for the particular project and will therefore not 'fluff up' too quickly during work. There are many suppliers of thread throughout the country besides those mentioned above, many of whom advertise in *Embroidery*, the quarterly journal of the Embroiderers' Guild.

Frames
The Royal School of Needlework can supply slate frames with 18, 24, 28 and 36-inch webbing.

The above-mentioned firms welcome overseas orders, but in America requirements may be obtained direct from:

Bucky King, Embroiderers Unlimited, 121 South Drive, Pittsburgh,
   Pennsylvania 15238
American Crewel Studio, Box 553 Westfield, New Jersey 07091,
and *Appleton Brothers of London, West Main Road, Little Compton,*
   Rhode Island 02837.

Part V What is owed to canvas work of the past

Most of us visit a museum at some time or other. Sometimes on these visits we consciously observe what has been achieved in the past in the use of a certain technique, but very often the significance of what we see registers only in our subconscious minds. When we experiment with our own work for a time before returning again to works of previous centuries, we may realise that a certain amount of what we are doing has a direct link with the past, but the fact is that, whether by conscious or unconscious process, many of the basic ideas of contemporary work had their origin many centuries before. It would indeed be interesting to see what sort of canvas embroidery might be produced by someone who had not had the opportunity to inspect anything of a previous age.

The following photographs have not been selected for the purpose of providing a history of the subject or to depict a steady progression through the past to the present day. These examples from bygone days do not therefore form the first section of the book, but have been placed last in order to show that all the work of the contemporary section, even when this contains experiment and originality, does owe a great deal to pieces that may be of considerable antiquity. These nine works do perhaps illustrate some of the most intriguing treatments to be found and may suggest many fields of inspiration other than those in the contemporary section of the book, where once again a varied and completely new approach can be achieved.

Many of the more familiar aspects of canvas work are already known to the keen embroiderer. Under this heading must immediately be placed the widely used tent stitch. It is known in works of the Middle Ages and occurs in the ecclesiastical English work of 1250–1350 (*Opus Anglicanum*) and can be seen on examples such as the Syon Cope in the Victoria and Albert Museum, London, thought to be fourteenth century but now known to be later, which has an orphrey and border chiefly in tent stitch. This, as with many succeeding generations of tent stitch, does not represent an unusual use. The wealth of canvas embroidery that was produced in the late sixteenth century, the Elizabethan period, consisted of beautiful table carpets, wall hangings of classical or biblical subjects, coverlets, cushion covers and so on, but there was very little variation of technique and few diversions from tent stitch (petit point) save for the fairly frequent occurrence of cross stitch (gross point), the latter being the common technique for many eastern carpets. This is true too at the height of canvas work of the late seventeenth century and early eighteenth

147 Detail of mid-seventeenth century purse ▶

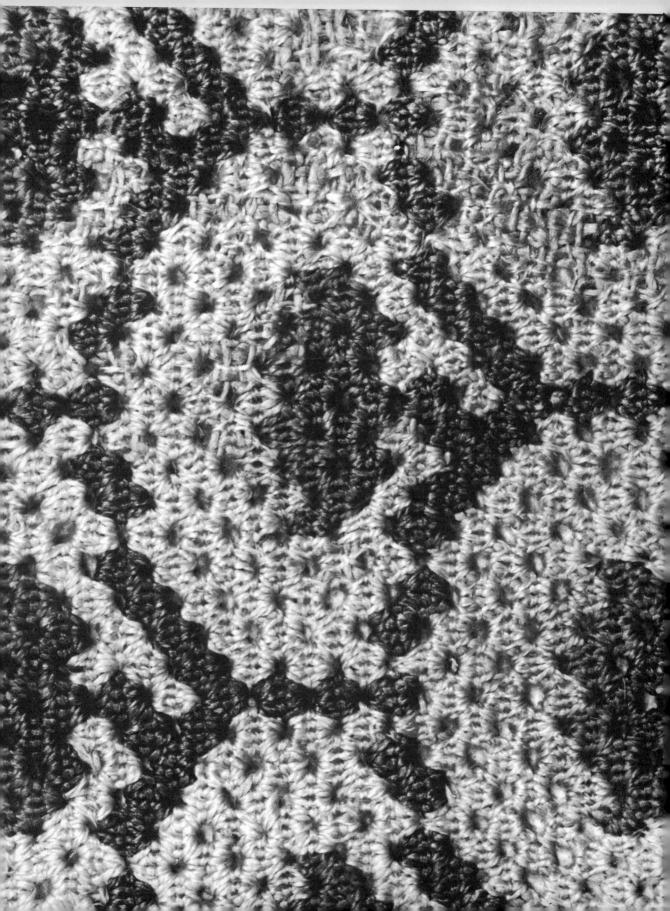

century with the addition of a different dominating subject: that of chair coverings. Once again there is little in the way of unusual technique except in a few examples such as stool top in the Victoria and Albert Museum, which experiments with the use of different thicknesses of wool causing varying amounts of relief. The most noticeable variations are the brightly coloured bands and flowers of florentine stitch in the upholstery of the time.

Experiment did, however, occur in a minority of works, one of which is the late seventeenth-century group of hangings known as *The Hatton Garden Hangings*, now in the Victoria and Albert Museum. This contains an unusual variety of stitches for any one work. The many stitches included have undoubtedly influenced work of the present day. They in their turn were inspired by the past derived from independent origins in many different countries and usually from counted thread embroidery, mainly on handwoven linen, an example of which can be seen in the twelfth century Egyptian fragment in the Metropolitan Museum, New York. It is worked in a stitch closely akin to gobelin.

Another variation from the more usual discoveries in techniques can be found within the wide field of Berlin wool work of the nineteenth century, for apart from the quantity of the very typical all-over cross stitch type came the quite different use of a single thread canvas woven with gimp. It was made by covering a very fine linen thread with tram silk. This being pleasant in itself meant that the surrounding ground around the pattern was left unworked. It was in various colours and offers many ideas for variation in contemporary work.

Delightful uses of a difficult stitch, rococo, occur in articles such as a workbox of mid-seventeenth century in the Victoria and Albert Museum, and the small purse also mid-seventeenth century in the Maidstone Museum, a detail of which is shown in figure 147, both of which are precursors of the work illustrated in figure 54.

Other valuable and different approaches occur. Household articles have been frequently embellished with canvas work, but one that gives much food for thought is a small *Book of Psalms* of 1627, measuring about $3\frac{1}{2}$ inches by 2 inches, in Maidstone Museum where, as can be seen in the photograph (148), the craftsman has superbly combined silver thread with silk. About half-a-dozen equally beautiful book bindings with similar techniques can be inspected at the British Museum.

148   Cover to *Book of Psalms*, 1627 ▶

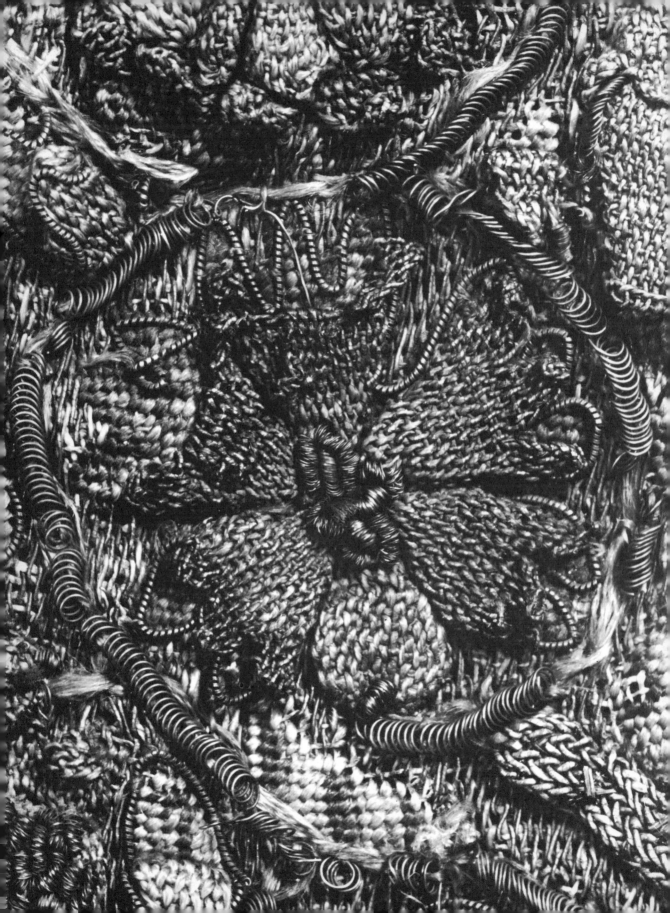

Canvas work has long been combined with other embroidery techniques. Plate 149 is a detail of a small bag in Maidstone Museum, which has tent stitch successfully combined with detached buttonhole stitch and coiled metal thread.

Plate 150 is a detail of a panel in tent stitch in Maidstone Museum, which also contains a typical seventeenth century technique that combines pearls and raised embroidery. Part I of the book contains many modern counterparts, in which the link with the past is sometimes intentional and sometimes not.

◀ 149

Plate 151 is a detail of a panel, English, early eighteenth century, in Maidstone Museum, which is an allegorical scene where all the motifs have been separately worked on canvas and later applied to a satin background. Figures 21, 22, 35 and colour plate 6 quite unconsciously have much in common with this work.

A fine example of a similar work in the Victoria and Albert Museum is a sixteenth century English cushion cover.

One often feels it is needless in certain instances to have to cover the entire background of a canvas work project, and after having worked on this aspect for some time it was a great joy to discover in the Victoria and Albert Museum an excellent example of a quite different sort. Plate 152 shows this unusual use of tent stitch in silk on a fine silk gauze leaving much of the background unembroidered as part of the design. It originates from Italy and is either late sixteenth century or early seventeenth century.

Figure 153 is a detail of a turkey work covering to a mid-seventeenth century English oak chair in the Victoria and Albert Museum. It is an intriguing technique that falls half-way between carpet knotting and what we now call velvet stitch. It has enormous possibilities and uses today and some of the experiments occur in plates 26, 71 and 72.

The detail of a nineteenth century border to a panel shown in figure 154 also belongs to the Maidstone Museum. This has been included because it seems to suggest countless ideas for freer approaches and uses on large projects.

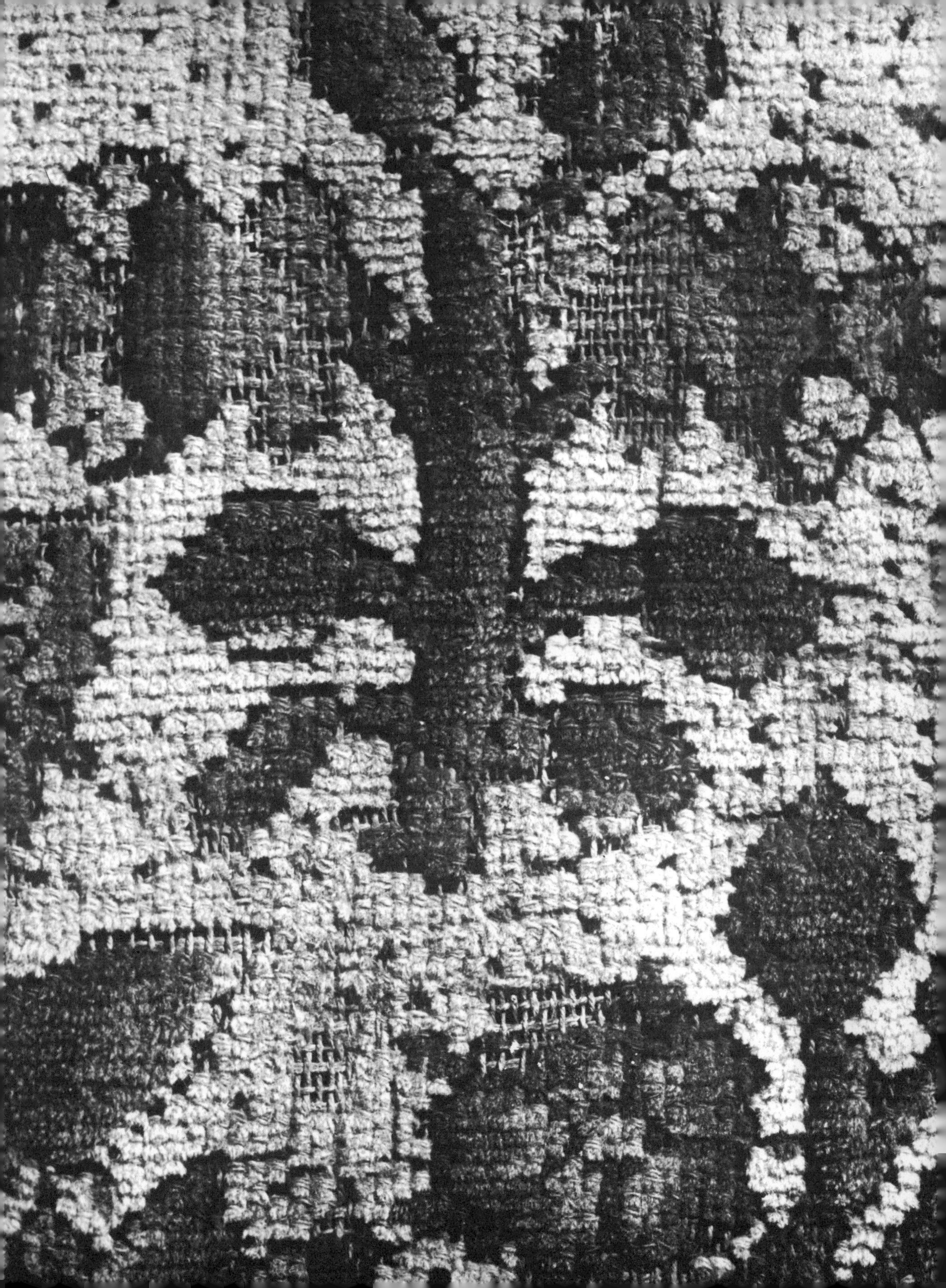

Figure 155 is a photograph of a beaded bag by Sophie Taeuber-Arp worked in 1916, and now in the museum at Basle. It has been selected for its possible inspiration for experiments in large areas of beading on canvas.

These plates of historical canvas embroidery not only show something of the more unusual and less well known aspects, but it is hoped will serve as an inspiration for new approaches. They represent only a small selection of the great variety of this work that can be found everywhere, and are set out to provide a starting point for searches and observation together with a view to linking them possibly with contemporary experiment and application.

◀ 154 Detail of nineteenth century border to a panel

Bibliography

The Uses of Air Photography, edited by J. K. S. St Joseph, John Baker Publications Ltd, London, 1966

Life under the Microscope. Dr Bedrich Boucek, Professor Jira Fiala, Academician Otto Jirovec, Spring Books, London

Forms and Patterns in Nature. Wolf Strache, Peter Owen, London. 1959

Creative Print Making. Peter Green, Batsford, London, 1964

Printmaking with Monotype. Henry Rasmusen, Chiltern Co., Philadelphia and New York, 1960

Pattern and Texture. J. A. Dunkin Webb Studio, London, 1956

Eye for Colour. Bernat Klein, B. Klein with Collins, London, 1965

Elements of Design. Donald M. Anderson, Holt, Rinehart and Winston, New York

The Painters Secret Geometry. Charles Bouleau, Thames and Hudson, London, 1963

English Domestic Needlework 1660–1860. Therle Hughes, Lutterworth, London, 1961

English Needlework. A. F. Kendrick, A. & C. Black, London, 1967

Catalogue of English Domestic Embroidery. J. Nevinson, H.M.S.O., 1950

Art d'Eglise (Belgian). Quarterly magazine.

Craft Horizons. Bi-monthly magazine.

Index

The numbers in *italics* refer to illustrations